God Does Care

God Does Care

The Presence of God in Our World

by

Wilfrid J. Harrington, O.P.

the columba press

This edition published in 1994 by
the columba press
93 The Rise, Mount Merrion, Blackrock, Co Dublin
in association with
Christian Classics Inc
Westminster, Maryland

Cover by Bill Bolger
Origination by Christian Classics
Printed in Ireland by
Genprint Ltd., Dublin

ISBN 1 85607 099 9

For Joan Glazier

Contents

Introduction

A Christian is one who is called to a way of life. Most of us are initiated into this way of life in our infancy, or we reach a time when we make a conscious decision to strive to live, seriously, or with some seriousness, a Christian life—or we drift away from that pattern. If we do persist in calling ourselves Christian, we do so for a variety of reasons. In the past, it seemed that Catholics found it hard to shed, wholly, their Catholicism. It is not at all clear that that is true today.

Our age does seem to be firmly marked by secularization. It does not appear to have much concern for God. At the same time, there is a thirst for meaning in life. This desire is a quest for God, even though it is not recognized as such. On the other hand, even when God is consciously sought, the quest may be misdirected; the god envisaged may not be truly God. This book is born of a conviction that God is not a distant or aloof God but is very near. Nor is the way of God some strange journey. I offer the following meditations to comfort and to encourage.

The plan of this book is straightforward. There is, first and foremost, a consideration of our yearning for wholeness—for salvation. At once the reality of God and our imagery of God emerge. We learn that God is God of humankind. He is found where there is goodness and a striving for the liberation of humankind. This calls for a critical assessment of religion. God is present in our history; he is found in the most ordinary aspects of human life. The path to God is the path of authentic humanness. Our secularized world has such need of God that our contemporaries may be more likely to find the true God than people of a more "religious" age.

There is the *graciousness* of our God. He is a Creator in love with his creation. He is a Parent, and we are all his favored children. He yearns to be loved as Parent by us. If our God took the generous risk of creating us as free beings, and has resolved to respect our freedom, he has paid a heavy price. Most painful to God is our ungraciousness. We have consistently painted him—even when ostensibly honoring him—in unflattering and repellent colors. It is needful to advert to this and to warn against false images of God.

Although we are children of God, we are, on the whole, rebellious children. We are conscious of sin. Our Parent calls us, gently and insistently, to *metanoia*, to a wholehearted turning to him. God knows us so much better than we know ourselves. He is eager to forgive. He waits, invitingly, for our turning to him. He *rejoices* over one who repents. Our God wants dialogue. He knows the strictures of our human lot, the frustration of our helplessness. When we cry out to him in anger, he understands—and smiles. Shouting at him is much better than maintaining an apathetic silence. He is most happy when, candidly avowing our sin, our ingratitude, we nevertheless come to him, trusting wholly in his forgiving love. Then we are his Children.

Paul assures us that "God was in Christ reconciling the world to himself" (2 Cor. 5:19). Our God is a God who so loves this human world that he gave his Son (John 3:16). The Son came to proclaim the rule of God: a new relationship of men and women designed to bring about a free and peaceful human society. That is why Jesus proclaimed good news to the poor—the needy of every sort, the outcasts. That is why he was friend of sinners, why he had table-fellowship with them. This conduct was to lead him to the cross.

In the Book of Revelation, Jesus is the Lamb—the Lamb *who was slain.* We are pointed to the Cross and to the paradox that is at the heart of Christianity. When Jesus bade his disciples, "It shall not be so among you" (Mark 10:43), his words reached beyond authority. He showed, supremely, through his life and death that, quite against the standard of the world, the Victim is the Victor. This follows on the radical living of the Christian Way as a way of *diakonia*—service.

Scriptural references in the text are taken from the *New Revised Version of the Bible,* Iowa Falls: World Bible Publishers, 1989.

1

Becoming Human

A yearning for salvation is a profoundly human desire. It is, in one form or other, at the core of every religion. We humans know ourselves to be flawed. We set goals before ourselves and fail to reach them. Time and again we find, to our dismay, that we are more frail than we had feared. We may seek to fool ourselves but cannot sustain the deception. We are unwhole but longing for wholeness. We look for salvation.

What is salvation? It is perceived in various ways; it has been made to mean many things. It has been made to seem ethereal, unreal. It has been presented as transcending humanness, even as denying humanness. This is tragic because salvation means nothing other than attaining perfect humanness. We *are* human beings, created in the

image of God; we are meant to *image* God. Our destiny is
to be human—as God understands humanness. The
corollary is that only with God can we reach full humanness.

Religion

Here, it is widely believed, is where religion comes in.
Religion, generally seen as humankind's relations with
God, is ostensibly a system and manner of life that unites
us with God, that enables us to be godly. Like all things
human, religion is subject to corruption. The temptation
of the religious person is to identify one's man-made world
with the world of God, and claim control over the holy. In
practice, religion may be a barrier to true union with God;
it may lock us into a narrow, impoverished way. Jesus
uttered his word, at once criterion and critique: "The sabbath was made for humankind, and not humankind for
the sabbath" (Mark 2:27). Paraphrased, it runs: "Religion
is in the service of men and women; men and women are
not slaves of religion." Wherever religion is burden, wherever it shows lack of respect for human freedom, it has
become oppressor, not servant. Authentic religion must
foster freedom. Of course, one has to understand freedom
correctly. In a Christian context, freedom is never license
to do as one pleases. Paradoxically, the ultimate freedom is
freedom *to serve.* "The Son of Man came not to be served

but to serve, and to give his life as a ransom for many"
(Mark 10:45). Here is the firm Christological basis of
authentic freedom.

Salvation

Salvation happens in our world, in our history.
Salvation comes from God but happens, as it must, in the
lives of human beings. It reaches into and touches every
aspect of human life. Otherwise it would not be salvation
of humankind. Salvation is not confined within the limits
of religion. Indeed, too often religion is and has been an
obstacle to salvation—the whole liberation of the wholly
human. And it is only where men and women are free to
be truly human that the human person becomes the image
of God. It is only so that the true being of God may be
revealed. Being image of God is not only the reflection of
God but the revelation of God.

Revelation of God occurs where the doing of good
brings about liberation, breaking the bonds that stifle
whatever is truly human. Revelation of God and, conse-
quently, salvation happen in a striking manner when
oppressive religious bonds are broken. God is most unam-
biguously revealed in human love. This accounts for the
New Testament emphasis on love of one another, love
even of the enemy. This explains the love commandment
of the Fourth Gospel. The Johannine Jesus is the Revealer.

If he insists "Love one another," it is because he is revealer of God.

None of this is pie-in-the-sky. Our faith-experience of redemption is lived out in finitude, in conditions that are not at all evidently redeemed. We are theoretically unable to reconcile the reality of redemption from sin and death with actual human suffering, with the troubled state of our world. Faith is the response to the situation. Faith does not save us from the darkness and the riddle, but it is the answer because it reaches, through the darkness and beyond the riddle, to the Son and to the Father.

God-Image

If authentic humanness is to be achieved with and only with God, it is obviously of vital importance that one's understanding of God be true or, at least, not overly flawed. Our talk about God is bound up with our world, bound up with talk about humankind. While we cannot *know* God, we may experience the presence of God. Because God is Creator, sustainer of all that is, there is no situation in which God is not present, no place in which he may not be found. This is why a believer can come to terms with situations that, humanly speaking, are meaningless and absurd—that remain absurd. The believer does not, in such circumstances, invoke the "will of God." To do so is meaningless. Human suffering and tragedy are never the will of God. What does matter is that God is never removed from our experiences.

To experience the presence of God, we must let God into our lives. And this means that we must accept ourselves, we must dare to be ourselves. For to accept ourselves as we are is to open the self to accepting God as he is. Coming to terms with one's self does not mean settling for mediocrity; it is not remaining where we are. We might apply the parable of the Wheat and the Weeds (see Matt. 13:24–30): "let both of them grow together until the harvest" (13:30). This parable is word of admonition: the final decision is at the harvest and is God's alone. But "wheat" and "weeds" are human beings, in this context members of a Christian community. The parable is a challenge to look at oneself, to see oneself. And if I recognize that I am "weed," I am not destined to remain such. I can become "wheat." Indeed, I am invited to become "wheat." It is what God desires of me.

God is God-for-us. The true God is God of love. God's love for us is not sentiment: it is active and efficacious love. Our response to God's love cannot be in word only; it must be in service. And the service God looks for is our service of one another. God's love is all-embracing, but it is not possessive. His respect for humankind is tireless. He *will* honor human freedom. Our response, then, should have something of the quality of God's love. It should be outgoing and delicate, sensitive to others, giving

them room to grow. The way of life is the way of loving
the Lord, of cleaving to him—and of being faithful to
what he asks. The way of life is the way of walking in the
way of God, which for us is the way of humanness. Who
would not choose life? This life is gift—and to recognize
the gift one must know the Giver. We need, more than
perhaps we realize, to have a true image of God. Too many
of us make do with a God who, if not a crassly false God,
is not yet the God who challenges our love.

> "The Lord is sweet, the Lord is sweet—O, hear,
> all you afflicted ones, be glad and sing
> with me a new psalm! I bring good tidings—
> taste of loving kindness: He is near
> the broken-hearted. Rising hope He brings
> the crushed in spirit—healing in His wings,
> Sun-Savior! Taste—the Lord is here—
> good, sweet . . . as bread and wine upon
> our tables!" So the old psalmist called.[1]

Jesus

For us Christians God is not an abstraction nor true
humanness, only an ideal. True, whole humanness has
been lived among us. Jesus of Nazareth, "the reflection of
God's glory and the exact imprint of God's very being,"is

one who had become "like his brothers and sisters in every respect" (Heb. 1:3; 2:17). Up to the launching of his brief ministry he had lived an uneventful life. During that public phase he was to rouse more opposition than support. He was not immune from suffering, not even from the agony of an atrocious and humiliating death. The fact that he was "without sin" (4:15) did not imply any lack of humanness. Sin—though we all are sinners—is *not* an intrinsic ingredient of humanness. It is a fall from humanness.

In maintaining that Jesus of Nazareth was wholly human, I am not suggesting that he was "merely" human. He is the one in whom God is wholly present, the one through whose life and deeds and words God has spoken his final word to humankind. As the human person in whom God is fully present, Jesus has defined God for us. All authentic religion is, in some measure, revelation of God. What is distinctive of Christian religion is that *Jesus* is revelation of God. He tells us who God is and what God is like: he is the God "made flesh" in Jesus. Traditionally, our theology has put the cart before the horse by striving to explain Jesus in terms of God. It is by accepting, totally, the humanness of Jesus of Nazareth that we, to the limit of our human intelligence, can attain knowledge of God. And it is by perception of the humanness of Jesus that we gain a right understanding of humanness.

Becoming Human

It has been well said: "None can say worse of God, than that his invitations are not in earnest."[2] The invitation of God, the call of God, comes to me not in signs and wonders but in the web and woof of every day. Here is where I find my God: where I am now, in what I do now. There is, indeed, a call that has—or is meant to have—the quality of prophetic call, such as the call to religious life. By its nature, it is relatively rare. One is concerned here and throughout with the invitation to live as child of God. God's call to us is, ordinarily, not something rare or special. It is a summons to the special task of being human and ordinary. That is challenge in plenty. Someone has said that holiness consists in doing ordinary things extraordinarily well. A sad by-product of religion is departmentalization. True, there are seasons and places that are "sacred." But this does not mean that all the rest is "secular." All that is good, all that is authentically human, is sacred. Sin is precisely denial or betrayal of the good, the truly human.

If "the human" is medium of divine revelation, there is an important proviso. God is to be seen in human freedom; the liberation of humankind is the way of salvation. Yet, God always transcends our world. He cannot be constrained by any manner of human progress.

[God] is indeed the source and the heart of all truly human movements of liberation and salvation, but he does not coincide with any particular historical liberating event, not even with the liberating exodus event of the Jewish people or the ministry of Jesus which created space, liberated men and women and forgave their sins. The name of God, for Christians symbolized in the name of Jesus Christ, can be misused not only by oppressors but also by liberators. This is the proviso which follows from the "divine way" in which he is a liberating God—liberating constantly by means of men and women, but at least in the end never in a purely human way.[3]

Self-Knowledge

Acknowledgment of a gracious God does not imply a lowering of standards. When I have convinced myself that God knows me so much better than I know myself, when I have simply and wholly accepted that God loves me for myself and as I am now and at every moment, then I will hear his invitation. Awareness of my shortcomings will not inhibit or depress me. It will spur me to do better, to be better. Response to the comforting assurance of God's love will not bring complacency but a willingness to respond. It will not matter if response is not as generous, as wholehearted, as I could wish. God will not ask of me more than I can deliver. And, if I fall, I can pick myself up again. Experience of my frailty will not dishearten. It will make me more appreciative of a love that is wholly undeserved, that does not count the cost.

Freedom

If I have really come to acknowledge that Prodigal Father of Jesus' parable (see Luke 15:11–32), that foolish God of Paul (see 1 Cor. 1:18–25), then I can taste freedom. I will be free of stifling preoccupation with self, free of crippling feelings of guilt. I can dare to be more open with others. And, perhaps most liberating of all, I will be free of restrictive bonds of religion. Worship and observance will find an important place in my life. My worship of a gracious God will not be duty but glad response. And observance will not be measured by obedience of rules and law but by practical acceptance of a lifestyle in keeping with my status as child of a beloved Parent. Response will not be calculated nor tinged by fear. It will be free. And life will be worth living.

The Cross

This is no soft option. Christians may be children of God but only on condition that they understand what this

means and live what it demands. The way of being a child
of God has been firmly traced by Jesus himself: "Anyone
who wants to be a follower of mine must renounce self,
take up one's cross and follow me" (Mark 8:34). Jesus
delivers a challenge, the challenge of his own way as Son.
Being a disciple is a serious business. Yet, taking up one's
cross is not at all to say that suffering is something
Christians should seek. Jesus did not seek suffering;
Gethsemane is proof enough. But suffering will be part of
Christian life as it was part of Jesus' life. The comfort is
that the following can be in tiny steps. God is patient. His
challenge is invitation. Faithfulness to one's way of life,
concern for others in whatever manner, the caring gesture,
the kind word—these add up. There will be heroes, the
few; there will be those whose way will seem ordinary,
drab—the many. Even in the things of God we are prone
to measure by worldly standards. The Lord does not over-
look the painful decision, the unspoken sorrow, the secret
suffering. There are surely many more saints than those
whom we honor as such.

It is fitting that the Cross has become the Christian
symbol—fitting, if it be understood. Sadly, it can be the
mark of a grim, unchristian religion. Rightly, it is the mark
of a love that will not count the cost. "God so loved the
world that he gave his only Son" (John 3:16). We must set
aside our "wisdom" and settle for the folly of God's love. If
we would listen to Paul and Mark (the New Testament

theologians of the cross), indeed to all the theologians of
the New Testament and to the theologians of our day who
are attuned to them, then, as Paul counseled his Galatians
(see Gal. 4:1–7; 5:1), we would cast aside the shackles of
legalism and rejoice in freedom, a Christian freedom ever
circumscribed by love. The Son of God came to serve. . . .
Freedom *to serve*—that is freedom indeed. And therein lies
the hope of humankind. Through the freedom of love we
can truly be children of the Father, can be our fully human
selves. We can be images, revealers, of God.

The Other

Accepting one's self reaches, necessarily, to accepting
others. That is the burden of Jesus' warning about seeing
the speck in the brother's eye while ignoring the plank in
one's own (see Matt. 7:3–5). It is only when I have come
to terms with myself, which means candid acknowledgment of my frailty and my failures, that I can fairly assess
others. To see myself as I am calls for humility. "Learn
from me; for I am gentle and humble in heart" (11:29).
Jesus, meek and humble, was a man of consummate
courage. While he would not dominate, he never shrank
from challenge. He challenged injustice. His view of injustice was distinctive. He could admonish: "Render to
Caesar what is Caesar's" (Mark 12:17). This gave Caesar
no carte blanche; the claim of God stands always para-

mount. It will be that Caesar oversteps his rights. Jesus would not condone violence. He countenanced resistance, yes—but passive resistance. When it came to it, he would not yield. He stood by his principles and steadfastly faced condemnation and death.

The Paradox

In his portrait of Jesus and in his related picture of discipleship—these are the concerns of his gospel—Mark seeks to present the paradox of Christianity. He shows that Jesus did not seek to capitalize on his influence (his initial success) or force himself on people. He did not match violence with violence but allowed himself to be taken. By human standards his cause was an abject failure: condemned by the religious authorities of his people, deserted by his own disciples, he died the death of a common criminal. Failure could not be more glaring. Therein lies the paradox of the Christian way. In reference to the style and exercise of civil authority Jesus had declared: "It shall not be so among you" (Mark 10:43). The declaration is of wider scope and reaches into other areas besides authority. It implies that, in many respects, Christian standards are not—or ought not be—standards of this world. But, in practice, what do we find? In the Christian churches of the Western world—Western Europe, North America—we have settled for a respectable Christianity. There can be no doubt that for a Paul and a Mark, a respectable Christianity is a contradiction in terms.

We have the lesson of Latin America. For centuries the official Church there had a cozy relationship with the political powers—often dictatorial regimes. In all that time we scarcely heard and rarely thought of a Latin American church. Then, after Vatican II there was a shocking development. Thousands of Christians in Latin America began to listen to Jesus. Think of it! And the Latin American church became front-page news. Christians had thrown down the gauntlet. They challenged the darkness of oppressive political regimes. Their challenge: *God's preferential option for the poor.*

These Latin American Christians continue to show that to be light of the world (see Matt. 5:14–16) is dangerous, very dangerous. They have suffered and died, in thousands. Their bitterest suffering has been lack of sympathy and support where they had, rightly, expected to find it. That, it seems, is the inevitable fate of their prophetic role. The fact remains: there is no manner of compromise between the way of Jesus and the way of the world—a world understood as a world opposed to gospel values and not just the necessarily untidy world of humankind. When we find ourselves in step with that other world it is time to ask: *Where* are we going? We may still be somewhere on the right road. By the measure of the gospel we have no grounds for complacency.

Being Christian

There is more than one way of being Christian. One need but look to the rich pluralism of the New Testament. It is a temptation of organized religion to construct a map with the "orthodox" road to salvation clearly defined. Alternative routes are, in this view, at best dead ends; at worst they head in quite the wrong direction. There are those who find comfort in the map and are helped on their way by it. There are others who trudge along, grimly. They find that though the map may be clear, the road turns out to be an obstacle course. There are some who find the map helpful in spots but who prefer to wander and explore. These people take religion seriously but preserve a sense of humor. They smile at self-importance and posturing. They are ready to follow their hearts. They are not awed by logic, because they know that God, the supremely free, is wondrously illogical. They are not browbeaten by law, because they know that God is the God of freedom. Perhaps, best of all, they do not take themselves too seriously—precisely because they know that God takes them with utter seriousness.

Two contrasting attitudes to religion were finely summed up by C. H. Dodd. In his classic commentary on Romans, in an allusion to a harshly legalistic text of Hebrews, he cites the Pauline outlook:

"It is an awful thing'" says the Epistle to the Hebrews
(10:31) "to fall into the hands of the living God."
Paul, with a finer instinct, sees that the really awful
thing is to fall out of His hands.[4]

The Luxury of God

Our Western world seems to some to be characterized
by rampant secularization. We bemoan the absence of
God. Many Christians tend to take a poor view of our
world. In truth, a pessimistic Christian is a contradiction
in terms. We ought to be incurably optimistic. "In the
world you face persecution. But take courage; I have conquered the world!" (John 16:33). What is encouraging is
the realism underlying this assurance. The promise is
uttered in the setting of a world that, in essence, was little
different from ours.

It is refreshing to hear a theologian who finds hope
and promise where too many can discern only ground for
discouragement. Edward Schillebeeckx maintains that in
the contemporary world the question of God is the most
open question of all, that the way to God is the most excit-
ing challenge. God is on the side of humankind. The
noblest task of humankind is to reveal the true God. God
is to be seen in whatever is authentically human. This is
why God was supremely present in the human person who
"went about doing good" (Acts 10:38). Our world not

only needs God but may be poised to acknowledge and
manifest God. And this because our world may be conditioned to acknowledge that God is pure gift—our ultimate luxury.

> Precisely in this Western social climate of secular-
> ization and religious indifference, of the spread of
> science, technology and instrumental thinking
> in terms of means to an end, the question of God
> becomes the freest and most gratuitous question
> that one may ask, and the way to God also
> becomes the freest career to choose. If within
> this context we look for points of expectation in
> human experience, echoes, traces or even held-
> back sounds which betray or suggest God's exis-
> tence, his free presence within a hair's breadth of
> us, then in our own time they might perhaps be
> found, be seen or heard, in the capacity of human
> beings to love without having a reason to; in that
> case we should perhaps have to look on the level of
> our human creativity, of feasts and celebrations,
> of generous self-giving and self-transcendence,
> though in the form of non-alienating self-empty-
> ing in favor of "the other." In such a context God
> would then be experienced by believers as pure
> gift, even pure freedom; every day new; without
> any reason.

God is not there as an "explanation" but as a gift. The idea which people are so fond of these days, that God is "the condition of the possibility" of human subjectivity, has taken not only the heart but also the "logos" out of all belief in God and theology. By contrast, the post-modern "we do not need God" is precisely the supreme luxury of any human life. It is precisely that which a person "needs." Thus for believers God is the luxury of their life—our luxury, not so much our cause or our final goal, but sheer, superfluous luxury. The oppressiveness of a scientific technological society calls for such a God.

In this sense God is more than necessary—but without becoming a function of our humanity. Therefore we also know ourselves called to a love which dares "the useless," the superfluous, the unnecessary. It is a matter of our making clear to men and women something of God's completely gracious and saving, gratuitous nearness which never leaves us in the lurch, not even when we leave him in the lurch. *Dieu a besoin des hommes,* God needs men and women, not in order to be God but in order to be a God of men and women. God himself determines in all freedom who he is and also who he wants to be for us. And on the basis of the Christian and religious tradition of experience we experience God as someone who opts for being as opposed to not-being, good as opposed to all evil. God is not on our side, as old political theologies often used to say; he is on the side of what is good, and that also means good for human beings. And it is important for us too to begin to stand on this side instead of taking God over.[5]

Conclusion

"This is eternal life: to know you, the only true God, and Jesus Christ whom you have sent" (John 17:3). It makes, literally, a world of difference whether one's God is the true God or a distorted image of that God. This matters all the more when one takes God seriously. The God I worship and serve has, necessarily, a dominant impact on my life. The quality of my worship, the manner of my service, shape my life. Is my worship a duty, faithfully but grimly rendered? Is my service the loveless service rendered to a taskmaster? There is no doubt that religion had been cast and lived along such lines. This is surely not what our religion is meant to be. Yet, it will be such if our perception of God is awry.

2

Creator and Parent

Our God is Creator. We are his creatures. There, already, is relationship. The quality of the relationship depends on the nature of the Creator. It could, conceivably, be a relationship of domination and subservience. Too often, indeed, it has been so imagined and presented. That must be when God is regarded, wholly or primarily, as an authority figure. Where there is another, different, perception of God as loving and gracious, creaturehood will be assessed accordingly. And when God is perceived as a vulnerable God, there is transformation. Now the relationship becomes one of Parent and child. God is still Creator, and very much God. He is a God who does not need slaves; he is a Father who desires children. This is the God preached by Jesus Christ, the God manifested by

Jesus Christ. He is a God perfectly recognizable in the Old Testament.

Gracious Creator

In the first eleven chapters of Genesis we have, arguably, the most theologically rich text in the Old Testament. There we learn much of our God and of ourselves. The creation stories of Genesis 1 and 2 are late, as creation stories go. We find much earlier stories in extant ancient Near Eastern texts. Still, the biblical stories stand alone in that the one and only God, Yahweh, is Creator. Elsewhere, creation of our world results from conflict among gods. There is no conflict in our God. True, chaos is out there, always a potential threat, a chaos firmly held in check by the absolute Master of creation.

God set out, in whole freedom, to call a universe into being. In Genesis 1 a refrain runs through the litany of creation: "God saw that it was good"—leading to the climactic declaration: "God saw everything that he had made, and indeed, it was very good" (Gen. 1:31). Understandably, the "world" of the narrative, ostensibly the universe, is, in practice, *our* world, our earth. The "two great lights" (sun and moon) are in the service of day and night and seasons and, ultimately, humankind. The stars are little more than ornaments in our sky (1:14–18). "It is good": the Creator alone can say this of his creation because the Creator alone can see the whole of it. We cannot look upon our world and declare, with truth, "It is very good." We cannot blind ourselves to so much that is, to our eyes, far from good. Job understood this. When he sketched the facile authority of the Creator over chaos and the heavens and the great waters (Job 26:5–13), he exclaimed, in awe: "These are indeed but the outskirts of his ways; and how small a whisper do we hear of him!" (26:14).

Looked at in another way, God's statement that in his eyes all is very good opens up for us a heady perspective: the possibility and the prospect of full, unfettered joy in the gifts of creation. But, it also makes possible our suffering with a God who suffers with and for his creation. Our comfort is the assurance that the God who has the first word in bringing into being and sustaining his world will have the last word: "Behold, I make all things new" (Rev. 21:5).

Belief in God as Creator is good news. It tells us of God and humankind and of their relationship in the world. Creation faith accepts that God willed to create the world as it is and human beings as they are. It accepts, without remainder, that finitude—contingency—is an inevitable feature of created reality. God, the Creator, is divine, infinite. Whatever God creates must, of necessity, be nondivine, finite. Finitude of our world, and of humanity, is not a flaw; things could not be otherwise. In short, contingency is the essential characteristic of humankind and of the world. God is Creator, and what he creates is creature.

God is *gracious* Creator. He is not mean-minded. Today, we have a perception far beyond that of the biblical writers of the well-nigh incredible grandeur of his creation. We become more and more aware of the sheer vastness of the universe—a vastness that boggles the imagination. God has created with appropriately divine abandon. Our awe before the vast expanse of the universe leads to awe of the Creator. Paradoxically, this awe brings us comfort. We have the assurance that this Almighty Creator, with a near infinite universe within his ken, has whole concern for humans on our puny planet: "What is frail mortal that you are mindful of him, a human being that you care for him?" (Ps. 8:4).

God has *divine* concern for us. This is not only our comfort—it is a measure of the true divinity of our God. The psalmist grasped and expressed the gracious magnanimity of the Creator when, in a tone of awe, he exclaimed of God's creation of humankind: "You have made them a little lower than God" (Ps. 8:5).

In the Likeness of God

Human dignity is found in creaturehood. This is precisely because humankind—man and woman—is created in the image of God, created to stand before God. There is the desire of God—his need for a counterpart. "Let us make humankind in our image" (Gen. 1:26). God will not remain alone. He set out to design a creature who would correspond, one with whom he could speak and who might listen. In the biblical perspective, human beings are unique in that they are God's counterpart: their *raison d'être* is their relationship to God. In creation as we know it, God has dialogue with humans alone. Because God is a loving God, that dialogue is free. His counterpart will respond to him in freedom—or not at all. Humankind is God's image: his representative who administers the earth in his name (see Gen. 1:26–28). As the image of God, the human person is revelation of God.

Blessing and Task

Humankind receives a blessing: "fill the earth and subdue it, and have dominion" (1:28). The blessing sets up a special relationship between humans and their environment, and between them and the animal kingdom. Dominion carries heavy responsibility. The earth and everything in it and on it has been entrusted to humankind, but it remains God's property: "The earth is the Lord's and all that is in it" (Ps. 24:1). God has concern for all of his creation, not only for humankind. Humankind has authority, but true authority calls for pro-

found respect for the object of authority. It is of supreme
moment that the blessing does not reach to the exercise of
dominion over humans. God alone is Lord of
humankind—humans are meant to be brothers and sisters. Jesus faithfully followed this pattern with his discipleship of equals and its paradoxical shape of authority—
authority as *diakonia,* service. The domination that is the
hallmark of sin has no place in his scheme of things—
"it shall not be so among you" (Mark 10:42–45).

Humankind has a special task in our world. The transformation of the world, the development of a better and
more tolerable human society, has been placed in the
hands of contingent humans. We cannot expect God to
relieve us of our responsibility and its consequent prob-
lems. We may not shift this back to God. It is our task to
face up to and to strive with all the means at our disposal
to overcome suffering and evil. It is our service, one that
we perform in the presence of God. We shape our history,
but we are not masters of it. We have no control over the
future. God alone is Lord of history. We do our best
within the limits of our finitude—and leave the rest to
God.

Salvation

We are conscious of struggle in our world; we experience struggle within ourselves. We imagine that God and

evil are locked in combat. Nothing in our world would assure us that, in the last resort, good, not evil, will triumph. Faith in a benevolent Creator offers the only—and certain—assurance. The finitude of our existence is caught up in his world of creation. We are meant to be human beings in a sphere that is, simply, the world. It is futile to look for salvation beyond our creaturely existence. Christian salvation is salvation of and for human beings— men and women of flesh and blood. The goal of salvation is the creation of a free society for free human beings. Salvation is not, nor was it ever meant to be, the salvation of "souls." It is a matter of the healing, of making whole the person. It includes and involves society and the world of nature. It comprises eschatological, social, and political aspects.

Salvation has been understood—or misunderstood— in so many ways. It surely cannot mean being saved from our finitude and from everything that this finitude involves. Salvation means that, here and now, we strive to be human—in our mortality and in our suffering. If this is not so, then Jesus of Nazareth is not the *whole* human being that our faith acknowledges him to be.

God

Paradoxically, it is through perceiving the limitations of our world that we recognize the divinity of God. By the same token, it is how we come to evaluate the specific nature of humankind and of the world. Throughout the Bible, the fundamental sin, one repeated throughout history, is to seek to abolish the limitations of creaturehood. The challenge, and the way of peace and salvation, is to welcome our creaturehood. "To enjoy and love what is worldly in the world, is to enjoy and to love what makes God God."[6] *Gloria Dei vivens homo*—God's glory lies in the happiness and well-being of humankind in our world, which is God's world. And God is with us in our finitude and in our involvement in this finite world.

> In sum, what God is this? A God:
> Who calls into being: "Behold, it is very good";
> Who respects our freedom;
> Who yearns for dialogue;
> Who cares and grieves;
> Who invites us to bear the image of his Son
> —to be his CHILDREN.

Parent and Children

In Genesis 1, the creation of humankind is written about with admirable directness and succinctness: "God created humankind (*ha-adam*) in his own image, in the image of God he created them; male and female he created them" (1:27). The Yahwist told the story in his way (2:7). Yahweh molded a shape out of dust from the earth. When he had breathed life into that shape, behold, a human being! Formed of dust from the ground, the human form will return to the ground—a play on *adam* and *adamah* (ground); humankind is set, inexorably, on a course from birth to death. God made a home for *adam*—the man— and set a program for work: a trait and right of humanness. Yet, that adam is incomplete. "I will make him a helper as his partner" (2:18). "This at last is bone of my bones and flesh of my flesh" (2:23). Man now has a companion, a partner sharing life to the full. Now there is community—and now there is whole humanity. "It is not good that the man should be alone." Human living cannot be understood only in relationship to God. Community, a harmonious relationship between men and women, is God's purpose for humankind. The community of man and woman is the basic shape of community.

To Be Like God

Law, by nature, is impersonal; it may be as impersonal as a legal code that, in practice, will remain a closed book to most people. A command, on the other hand, is personal: it sets up a relationship between the one who utters the command and the recipient of the command. In

Genesis, God issues a command: "You may freely eat of every tree of the garden; but of the tree of the knowledge of good and evil you shall not eat" (Gen. 2:16–17). That command is an acknowledgment of human freedom. Humans can obey—or disobey. The temptation story (Gen. 3) brings matters to a head. The function of the *nahash,* a talking snake—a stage prop—is to focus attention on the command (see Rom. 7:9–11) and to spell out that disobedience is, in effect, a vain attempt "to be like God." It will remain the perennial human temptation. But to call it the desire to be "like God" is, perhaps, too blatant. What is in question is, firmly, that God is God and humans are creatures. The simple fact is that the Creator God cannot create God. What is created is, by definition, creature. We, as creatures, can achieve fulfillment *only in relation to* our Creator, not *without* him. Any human attempt to go it alone, to live without reference to God, is doomed to failure.

One realizes that sin is the *deliberate* rejection of a superior Power. It is an act of rebellion by which human beings take the place of God and make themselves arbiters of morality and conduct. At the same time, there is human effort and achievement that, if not undertaken with express reference to God, is not consciously in defiance of him. On the other hand, much is and has been done in the name of God which he certainly does not condone. What it all boils down to in the end is that we, as creatures, can

never break out of creaturehood. This is not because our
God is a jealous God—as the Genesis snake implied. He
is a gracious God who will not settle for being a benign
Creator who looks kindly upon his creatures. He will settle for nothing less than full Parenthood, with humans as
his beloved daughters and sons. Unhappily, the Cain and
Abel story (Gen. 4) shows that the brothers and sisters
have not learned the human lesson too well. Society is
meant to be people together in community. History, up to
the present, is a sad tale of failure. Happily, God is the
eternal optimist.

Limits of Humanness

The idea that Genesis 2–3 has to do with an "original
state," a state of original innocence, forfeited by sin—
thereby involving a "fall" into our present state—rests on
a misunderstanding of the text. The story is concerned
with human existence; it is not dealing with any historical
situation. The "primal sin" is found in the fact that
humans, in one fashion or another, do not want to accept
their own finitude. They hanker after omniscience and
immortality; they aim at being like God. This is because,
as we have observed, finitude is regarded as a flaw rather
than taken for what it is: a necessary and inescapable feature of our creaturehood. It is human destiny to be human
beings in a real world, a world that is wondrous but is also

a world of failure and suffering. The finitude of the world and of humanity is not the result of a fall from grace. Our belief in God as Creator does not deny the finitude of creation, nor does it distort contingency into sin or fallenness. God abides in and with the contingent, that is to say, the world with its limitations and humankind in its finite humanity.

Humans are called to responsibility for their conduct: "Where are you?" (Gen. 3:9). While humans cannot be made responsible for the origin of evil, humans remain answerable. The primeval story of Genesis looks to the human state as it exists in the lives of real men and women. The question faced there is: why is the human being, created by God, limited by death, suffering, toil, and sin? The question is not answered. The mystery of evil is left hanging—a mystery. The fact is that humankind is alienated from God—alienated but not cut off from God. Sin and death are part of human existence. Consciousness of nakedness had followed awareness of rebellion, awareness of guilt (3:7). God "clothed them" (3:21). The feeling of guilt is removed. God sent man and woman out into the world free of guilt feeling.[7]

The Grief of God

The story of the Flood (Gen. 6–9) is of major theological significance. It dramatizes the destructive nature of

sin and the reaction of God to sin. The episode of the
"sons of God and daughters of men" (Gen. 6:1–4) is
meant to mark a stage, far beyond that of the man and
woman of Genesis 3, in the futile human striving "to be
like God." What is in question is wholesale corruption—
to such a degree as to threaten human existence. God *has*
to do something about the situation, though his reaction
is grief and sorrow, and he unleashes the flood waters. Yet
the point of the story is: "God remembered Noah" (8:1).
Therein is the turning point: from a path of destruction
there is a turn to salvation. The story ends in hope and
promise: "I establish my covenant with you, that never
again shall all flesh be cut off by the waters of a flood, and
never again shall there be a flood to destroy the earth"
(9:11). Even more significant is the repeated statement in
the introduction and conclusion of the story. At the beginning "every inclination of the thoughts of their hearts was
only evil continually" (6:5). At the close, after the promise
that there will never be another Flood, the repeated observation is: "for the inclination of the human heart is evil
from youth" (8:21). God had decided to bear with
humankind's tendency to evil.

God and Sin

Throughout Genesis we are in the presence of myth:
the expression of universal truth. It is a paradigm of an

ongoing biblical concern. God represents infinite love and mercy and forgiveness. He wills the salvation of all. In fact, God would never launch a flood to destroy humankind. He is Creator, source, and sustainer of life; he is not in the business of destruction. The Book of Wisdom puts it aptly: "all existing things are dear to you and you hate nothing that you have created—why else would you have made it" (Wisd. 12:24). But . . . does that mean God is unconcerned with evil and sin? Obviously not. Here our limited understanding faces a daunting problem. How is one to portray the divinely loving forgiveness of God without conveying the false impression that he shrugs off sin as incidental? The beginning of an answer emerges when we understand that sin is not, and cannot be, a direct affront to God. Human sin, whatever shape it takes, is the betrayal of our humanness. Moreover, sin can be against our environment. And destruction of our world is sinful. We humans have sinned grievously against our animal cohabitants on this planet. Sin, whatever form it takes, is an affront to God's plan for his creation. And God as Creator grieves over sin.

If we are to speak of God at all, we must speak in human terms. But unfortunately, we tend to take anthropomorphism literally. We too readily lose sight of the fact that God-language is always *analogical.* We can, and do, make statements about God that make human sense. What is too often forgotten is that we cannot, and do not,

know God *in himself.* I may say with truth that God is a
loving God. I speak out of my experience of human love.
Though I have not an inkling of the *reality* of *divine* love,
my assertion is not meaningless. I may also speak of God
as a just God. Again, my experience of justice is human
justice: let the punishment fit the crime. Here we begin to
go hopelessly wrong. Our *just* God is reduced to our level.
Accordingly, we have come up with a God who condemns
sinners to hell—and rightly so! Objectively speaking, this
is blasphemy. The error is that what reasonably operates as
justice on the human level is taken to be operative in the
world of God. Consider the following statement: "God is
a just God, who deals with us fairly." By human standards,
impeccable. But . . . does any of us wish to be treated *fairly*
by God? Do we wish our God to deal with us as we *truly*
deserve? Surely, we hope to be treated with loving mercy.
And that is how our just God treats us—because divine
justice *is* mercy.

We are left with the problem of evil and sin. We cannot accept that God is unconcerned. There has to be a balance to the strange mercy of our God. So, there is the
notion of the "wrath" of God. This idea of God oscillating
between wrath and mercy is a hopeless human attempt to
find balance where, in divine terms, there is no balance to
be struck. We ask the question: how can we reconcile
God's mercy with God's justice? Like every human question we ask of God, it is a mistaken question. The first

Christian theologian got it right: "Has not God made foolish the wisdom of the world? . . . God's foolishness is wiser than human wisdom" (1 Cor. 1:20, 25). Too many later theologians misunderstood. Let us settle for a foolish God.

The comfort is that the foolish God is determined to put up with his wayward children. God, in creating humankind, took a risk—and paid the price. He would respect, respect utterly, the freedom of his children. Sadly, he would come to observe that the thoughts and inclinations of humans are perverse. Yet, he has determined that "never again shall there be a flood to destroy the earth." He will bear with humankind, however evil their bent. He will have the last word. He will because he is God of salvation, and human salvation is all about becoming thoroughly human. And that means becoming truly child of God.

Conclusion

God is a gracious Creator who loves his creation. He has created freely, and with abandon. We need look no further than our own planet. The author of the Book of Wisdom wrote: "The greatness and beauty of created things give us a corresponding idea of their Creator" (Wisd. 13:5).

In creation, as we know it, humankind is God's masterpiece. He has put the earth in our care. He has, with divine magnanimity, made us free, challenging us to responsibility. He has, with divine graciousness, called us to be his children. What has been our response? Novelist Paul Gallico asks:

> Supposing God *had* made man, not in His own image, but in some reflection of His own love and spirit and turned him loose on earth to work out his own destiny. Must not His heart, must not any great creative, all-embracing heart be wrung with compassion for what His children had turned out to be?[8]

There is grief and sadness in the heart of God. There is no wrath, no anger. Only in our perversity do we imagine an angry God. After all, children, especially teenagers, tend to regard the care and concern of parents as oppressive. With regard to our Parent, we have been rebellious teenagers. With infinite patience he bears with us, not infringing on our freedom, but respecting our dignity. He is saddened at seeing us enslave ourselves to other gods. He is saddened at the harm we have done: to ourselves, to others, to the whole of his earthly creation. He is grieved at the sheer burden of sin that weighs upon us. He is constantly calling out to us: "Here am I, here am I" (Isa.

65:1). He waits for our response, waits not only in
patience but with divine compassion.

But . . . is this truly the God we acknowledge and worship? I have become increasingly and painfully aware that,
for many who do profess to believe in God, their God is
an aloof figure: often unattractive and even oppressive. It
is not superfluous to turn our attention to false images of
God and how they blind us. It is a reflection on the commandment: "You must have no other gods before me"
(Deut. 5:7; see Exod. 20:3).

3

No Other Gods

alse Images

We have always been tempted to construct a god in our image. And we have attempted to manipulate God. People may have gods in their lives—they may not recognize them as such, but they worship them. It seems more serious when they are false images of the true God. God deserves better than the insult of ungracious caricatures. Let us consider the harmful effect of inadequate and hurtful concepts of God.

Idolatry

The most explicit and self-confident Old Testament texts dismissive of idolatry are post-exilic. This is not surprising. Before the Exile, Baal worship in particular seriously threatened Yahwism. After the Exile, that threat was no more. Now there was a firm—if complacent—dismissal of false gods. Isaiah delights in ridiculing the pseudo-deities of other nations (see Isa. 41:21–29; 46: 5–7; Jer. 10:1–16). For instance, in Isaiah, after yielding building material and fuel, a felled tree has a piece left over, fit for nothing except to be carved into an idol (44:9–20). The polemic reaches its climax in the Book of Daniel (Ch. 14). There, idolatry is openly mocked in a pair of rather unkind skits. More theological—and therefore more significant—is the satire on idols (see Wisd. 13:10–15:17), inspired by earlier texts. Here, idolatry is not only acknowledged to be of human origin, it is said to be the source of all human malaise: "For the worship of idols not to be named is the beginning and cause and end of every evil" (Wisd. 14:27).

In the New Testament, we see Paul's understanding of the human condition: everyone is subject to some lordship, to some power, which one must serve. The primal sin was to cast off the lordship of God, to seek to be "like God" (Gen. 3:5). It is the perennial human temptation. The irony is that rejecting the lordship of God does not remove us from all other lordships. Indeed, the root of human sin is to replace the lordship of God with the dominance of some other one or thing. This is the background of Paul's assertion in Romans (1:18–23), where he echoes the Book of Wisdom. (Here he has pagan Gentiles in mind; he accuses Jews of a more subtle form of idolatry.)

When Paul speaks of the "wrath of God" being revealed against the wickedness flowing from idolatry (Rom. 1:18), he insists that the wrath that God visits on sinful humanity is manifest in allowing humanity to have its own way: God "gave them up" to the consequences of their rebellion (Rom. 1:24, 26, 28). God "punishes" by giving us the freedom to do whatever we desire. For, having deliberately created free beings, God scrupulously respects human freedom. But, having freed ourselves from his benign lordship, we become slaves of other "lords." Humans worship at the altars of many idols.

Idolatry is not only a matter of false gods. As far as contemporary Christians are concerned, if the God one worships is falsely perceived, then one's worship is, in some sense, idolatry. It may not be conscious or deliberate idolatry, but it is tainted all the same. The fact remains that false images of God abound.

A Remote God

"We believe in one God, the Father, the Almighty." It is often the case that this confident credal statement enshrines a serious misconception. To proclaim that one believes in God is not enough. What matters most is the kind of God in whom one believes. The title "Father" conveys no consistent image of God. The qualification "Almighty," acknowledging God's sovereignty over creation, tends to veil the truth that his power is displayed above all in the cross of Jesus Christ— "the power of God and the wisdom of God" (1 Cor. 1:24). The fact remains that too often God is perceived exclusively as an authority figure. And strangely, although he is presented as gravely offended by human sin, he has also been presented as unaffected by human suffering.

We speak of God anthropomorphically, in human terms. We speak of God in metaphor. Since God is personal for believers, we speak of God in terms of human personality—the only personality we know. We speak of God in analogies. We can indeed say something about God. We can and do rightly say that God is a person, an intelligent being; he is good. But we do not know *divine* intelligence and *divine* goodness. And when we use metaphor, we must take care to balance one metaphor against another. Unfortunately, in practice, we are selective in our choice of metaphor.

The Law-Giver

If Paul saw idolatry as the bane of Gentile civilization, he came to view the Mosaic law as the bane of Jewish life. The problem with law, as he came to understand, is that fulfillment of it led to the false confidence that one had achieved a valid relationship with God. The Pharisee of Jesus' parable is an eloquent case in point: "God, I thank you that I am not like other people" (Luke 18:11). The law had come to be regarded not as pointing beyond itself to the God who rectifies our relationship with him (who *justifies*), but as the instrument by which we bring about that right relationship. Observance of law blinded one to the truth that justification is, solely, God's achievement: "justified by his grace as a gift" (Rom. 3:24).

If the way of life that is right with God is perceived as meticulous observance, then God will be perceived as law-giver and law-enforcer. Such a God is to be feared. He is the God of the elder son of Jesus' parable: "Lo, these many years I have served you, and I have never disobeyed your command" (Luke 15:29)—a son addressing his father! Worship of such a God would foster legalism, with its crippling sway. Paradoxically, the attitude can lead to manipulation of God: just the danger that Paul had envisioned—God seen as owing us salvation because we have been faithful.

God of Wrath

Closely related to the idea of God as law-giver is the idea of the God of wrath. Admittedly, there does seem to be scriptural warranty for this—not only in the Old Testament but also in the New Testament (if sparingly) we have reference to the "wrath of God" (e.g., John 3:36; Eph. 5:6). But it is significant that nowhere is it written that "God is wrathful." Only once does Paul write of the "wrath of God" (Rom. 1:18)—a traditional formula. Translators considered the noun *orgē,* which means "anger"; in biblical Greek that implied a reaction of the divinity to our sin. It seemed better to retain the archaic phrase "wrath of God"; the word "anger" might, mistakenly, suggest that God is angry with men and women. *Wrath* is impersonal: it means the effect or consequence of sin. It denotes cause and effect in a moral universe.

God is *not* ever angry or wrathful with humankind—not even with sinful humankind. Yet, God has consistently been presented as grossly offended by human sin: he will have reparation, otherwise he must punish. This is surely not the God of Jesus. His God grieves over our abuse of freedom, over the dire result of human sin. But sin does not affect God in himself; it hurts God in his creation. He grieves over the havoc sin wreaks in his world and on his beloved children. It is humans who, thinking of God in human terms, imagined the "wrath" of God.

A Male God

Nowadays it is not uncommon to find God referred to as "Mother." The designation is not inappropriate.

Because the Bible itself comes out of and reflects a patri-
archal culture, it tends to be androcentric, male-centered.
The predominant biblical metaphors for God are taken
from male experience, with God being depicted as father,
warrior, king, and so on. At the same time, there is an
intriguing openness to the use of female imagery with
God being imaged as birth-giving woman and loving
mother (see Deut. 32:18; Isa. 42:14; 66:13).

In point of fact, it makes as much sense to refer to God
as Mother as it does to call God "Father." God is neither
male nor female; God stands apart from such categories—
God is transcendent. To call God "Father" is to acknowledge that God is the source of our being, of our life, in a
manner that is, in some way, comparable to our parents'
role: they conceive us and care for us. In that sense, God
is Parent, but we do not *know* what divine "parenthood"
might mean—except that it must outstrip, infinitely, in
graciousness, the most lovable human parental relationship. It is due to linguistic convention (framed by patriar-
chal standards) that God is called "Father" and is spoken
of in male terms. Feminist theology alerts us to the truth
that the basic relationship is that of parent-child. The
image of God, we are told in Genesis, is found in whole
humanness: male and female together (Gen. 1:27). Still,
there is the pervasive conviction that God *is* male. Women
have paid, and continue to pay, a high price for this man-
ifestly mistaken perspective.

Blinding Effects

Idolatry

Idolatry is not only a phenomenon of the ancient past
or a feature of primitive cultures. In theological terms, it is
not absent from our modern world. While our eyes may
be opened to discern idols so that we may turn from them,
it is more difficult for us to recognize that we may, in reality, worship a false God.

As creatures, we humans are subject to lordship.
Ideally, this is the benign lordship of a gracious Creator.
But we are sinners, and sin, at the deepest level, is rebellion. The Yahwist was right in his diagnosis. The temptation: "you shall be like God" (Gen. 3:5) had the consequence of striving for independence from God. It is not
that God does not wish us to be *free*—God does. We can
be truly free *only* within the limitations of creaturehood.
God is not free to create God. Human freedom is the freedom of a creature. Limitation is not arbitrary but wholly
in the nature of things.

When we, in effect, shrug off the lordship of God, we
leave space for another lordship. We worship at the shrine
of some idol. The idol may wear many faces. It may be
power, wealth, sex, drug dependency. . . . In our sophisti-
cated world the prevalence of astrology is ironical. We
extol human freedom, untrammelled freedom—and

declare ourselves pawns of astronomical forces! According to the New Age movement, we live in the age of Aquarius. One could go on, but Paul said it best: "Although there may be so-called gods in heaven and on earth—as indeed there are many 'gods' and many 'lords'—yet for us there is one God . . . and one Lord, Jesus Christ" (1 Cor. 8:5–6).

A Remote God

Whatever one believes of idols, false images of God are more insidious and, ultimately, more harmful. We have noted some false or flawed impressions. Here we may sketch some unhappy effects. In reply to surveys, most people acknowledged that they believe in God. If pressed, many would admit that this God is an aloof and distant figure. He seems to have no impact on—and little interest in—his creation. For that matter, this concept of God goes hand in hand with a view of creation that regards it as a single moment: God created, and withdrew—an absentee monarch. It is true that God is not a being within the universe: he is the transcendent Creator who exists outside of creation. Yet he sustains his world from within. Creation is thus an ongoing process.

I cannot know God in himself. I know God through the conviction that I am loved, and that I am being loved. It is evident that a perception of God as distant and aloof makes it difficult, if not impossible, to have an assurance

of being loved. At best I could only cling to a belief in the
existence of a Creator. I would lack the living faith in a
Presence that could be my motivation and sustenance.
"You shall *love* the Lord your God." My God must be *lovable*. Otherwise the God I worship is not the true God
who loves me beyond measure for myself and as myself.
And my life is immeasurably poorer.

The Law-Giver

Here is a God prominent in our western tradition. He
lays down inflexible laws and goes by the book. He is a
God who casts a censorious eye on human conduct. He is
a God gravely offended by human sin. Here, indeed, one's
perception of sin is revelatory of one's perception of God.
In the Latin tradition, sin is crime: we break the commandments. We used to speak of the *tribunal* of penance.
In this model, God is seen as judge: he hands down a sentence, he demands reparation. In the Greek tradition, following Irenaeus, sin is sickness—to be healed: God is
Healer. This is no trivializing of sin (surgery, major or otherwise, is not pleasant), but the image of God as Physician
is so much more comforting. Unhappily, our judicatory
God holds the stage and has colored our moral theology
(perhaps, more truly, our moral casuistry) and our penitential practice. Worship of such a God would be meticu-

lous observance. Some of us will recall the tyranny of
rubrics—regarded as matters of serious moment! We recall
the obligation of prayer under pain of grave sin—surely,
this is a blatant contradiction in any Christian context. No
wonder there was such attention to scrupulous behavior.

It seemed not to have mattered that Jesus declared:
"The sabbath was made for humankind, and not
humankind for the sabbath" (Mark 2:27). Decoded, this
reads: Religion is for men and women, not men and
women for religion. Edward Schillebeeckx's observation is
perceptive and appropriately scathing:

> There is something subtle and killing in a particu-
> lar kind of virtue. The subtle vice of "perfection"
> has not yet disappeared from church life. People
> defend so-called unassailable laws, and in so doing
> injure already vulnerable fellow men and women.
> Jesus showed that up. The effect of this zeal is
> often to deprive men and women of room to
> breathe. Jesus opposes worldly practice when the
> law has the effect of excluding the other person. If
> the law reduces people to despair, it forfeits all
> authority. For Jesus, the poor and the outcast are
> the criterion of whether the law is functioning cre-
> atively or destructively, as the will of God for the
> benefit of men and women.[9]

God of Wrath

"God condemns sinners to hell." Throughout most of
Christian history, it was believed that God acted so.
Perhaps there are still Christians who believe God is prepared not only to hand down a sentence (lasting for eter-
nity!) but is willing to include eternal torture. Hell has
been presented this way in works of "piety" and in countless sermons—yet surely the statement is blasphemy. For
that matter, the popular perception of purgatory is even
more disturbing; people speak of the "poor souls"—even
of the poor *forgotten* souls. The assumption is that souls
may be bailed out of a purgatorial jail. But if no bail is
posted, then the unhappy "soul" will serve the full sentence. Not much "preferential option for the poor" there!
What is troubling are the lurid pictures of hell so earnestly
painted by mission preachers of the past and the legalistic
purgatory that conveys an unsavory, even repellent, image
of God. It may be that this image was not clearly perceived, but it surely lurked in the background. Any way
one looks at it, here is a God to be feared. And with such
fear there is no room for love.

A Male God

Our God-language, including the God-language of
Scripture, is emphatically male. Our God-image is andro-

morphic. The widely held corollary is that maleness reflects God in a way that femaleness cannot. If this were only theory, it would merely be ridiculous. In practice, the attitude has sustained the domination of men and the subordination of women, not only in society at large but tragically in the churches, too. Divine transcendence is compromised when it is maintained that God is more appropriately represented as male rather than female.

Jesus addressed God as Father—indeed, more intimately, as *Abba*. He thereby expressed their relationship in the conventional language of his concrete human state. This tells us not only of his personal relationship with God but the rich meaning of fatherhood in his Hebrew tradition. This aspect has serious theological implications. But the use of the title "Father," even by Jesus, does not mean that God is, in any sense, *male*. Appreciation of analogical language reminds us that we do not know what it means for God to be "Parent." It surely does not mean that God is male—or female, for that matter. To wield the alleged maleness of God as a weapon of domination is perverse. Macho God is an idol.

Conclusion

It might be argued that the more insidious enemy of God is not atheism but religion. Most atheists reject not God but the travesty-God presented by religion and by the

conduct of those who profess to serve God. The true athe-
ist, the one who calmly and deliberately rejects the very
possibility of a Supreme Being, has to be a person of
courage. To struggle through life without any light at all at
the end of the tunnel is challenging, but better that than a
life bolstered by trust in a false God. That is bad enough,
but what is intolerable is the foisting of false gods on others. In the history of religion, to our day, the fostering of
false gods has devastated, and is devastating, countless
lives.

The fact remains that false images of God abound—
not least among believers. God protests any manipulation
of him. He suffers and shares the pain inflicted in his
name on the weak and the vulnerable. So many spirits
have been broken, so many lives have been shattered—in
the name of God. Throughout history, even to this day,
God has been dishonored. He has been *wearied* beyond
measure. Because too often, and with frightening consis-
tency, religious observance has been the denial of, or sup-
pression of, human values. And any depreciation of
humanness is denial of the God of humankind.

4

God of Forgiveness

God is gracious, but his children have been less than gracious. Sin is pervasive. We stand in need of forgiveness. We must open our hearts to a forgiveness that is freely offered—to be received in freedom. We must turn to our Parent.

Repentance and Forgiveness

Like the call to conversion, repentance is a central theme of both the Old Testament and the New Testament. A preliminary glance at the relevant terms shows this. In the Old Testament the most frequently used term is *shub*: to turn away from evil and turn back to God. The Greek equivalent, *epistrephō,* similarly means to turn from wickedness—to turn to God. The New Testament does take up *epistrephō* to describe conversion, but prefers *metanoia*: a change of heart. For that matter, both terms signify a radical turning about of the whole person. In both the New and Old Testaments, the call to conversion always denotes a desire to return to the Lord and a yearning for his friendship.

That humanity has turned from God in sin gives the background to the biblical call to repentance. Various penitential practices were developed to implore the forgiveness of God for both personal and collective sin. There were ascetical practices: fasting, wearing sackcloth and ashes. There were penitential prayers, especially communal confession of sin:

> The Israelites cried to the Lord: "We have sinned against you, because we have abandoned our God and have worshiped the Baals." (Judg. 10:10)
> So [Israel] gathered at Mizpah . . . and fasted that day and said there: "We have sinned against the Lord." (1 Sam. 7:6)

Prophetic Call

The prophets' message of conversion challenged superficial ritual. Amos, for instance, was an uncompromising champion of justice. He castigated the disorders that prevailed in an era of hectic prosperity during the reign of Jeroboam II (783–743) in Israel. To Amos, the symptoms of social decay were glaring. Wealth, concentrated in the hands of a few—the leaders of the people—had corrupted its possessors. Oppression of the poor was rife. The richly endowed national religion, with its elaborate ritual, induced a comfortable, self-righteous atmosphere. The prophet set out to shatter this dangerous complacency. He did not mince his words.

> Seek good, and not evil, that you may live;
> and so the Lord, the God of hosts, will be with
>   you . . .
> Hate evil and love good, and establish justice in
>   the gate;
> it may be that the Lord, the God of hosts,
> will be gracious to the remnant of Joseph.
> (Amos 5:14–15)

Centuries later, Ezekiel struck a similar note, with deeper feeling:

> Cast away from you all the transgressions that you have committed against me, and get yourselves a new heart and a new spirit! Why will you die, O house of Israel? For I have no pleasure in the death

of anyone, says the Lord God. Turn, then, and
live. (Ezek. 18:31–32)

From Amos to Ezekiel, the doctrine of conversion had
steadily developed. It is not surprising, then, that the God
of Jesus is, firmly, this gracious God.

Call of Sinners

Virtually everything that the early Church remembered about John the Baptist had to do with repentance in
view of imminent judgment. But with Jesus we have a different emphasis. There is the summary statement that
Jesus preached repentance in view of the nearness of the
kingdom: "The time is fulfilled, and the kingdom of God
has come near; repent and believe in the good news"
(Mark 1:15). While there is a summons to repent, it is
surely not the whole message. Indeed, there is not a significant body of reliable material that *explicitly* attributes
to Jesus a call for general, or for national, repentance in
view of the coming kingdom. What is surprising is that,
while looking for the restoration of Israel, he did not follow the majority and urge the traditional means toward
that end: repentance and return to observance of the law.

Jesus himself was not primarily a preacher of repentance; he proclaimed the imminent coming of the kingdom as *salvation.* The parables of God seeking the lost

(Luke 15:3–6, 8–9), once Luke's conclusions (15:7, 10) are removed, can be seen as focused not on repentance but on God's initiative and action. The one distinctive note that we can be certain marked Jesus' teachings about the kingdom is that it would include the "sinners." There should be no confusion about the basic meaning of the term "sinners" in the gospels. It comes from the Hebrew *resha'im*—the wicked: those who sinned wilfully and did not repent. They renounce the covenant. Jesus saw his mission as being to "the lost" and the "sinners," that is, to the wicked. He was also concerned with the poor, the meek, and the downtrodden. If there was conflict, it was about the status of the *wicked*: "This fellow welcomes sinners and even eats with them!" Jesus was accused of associating with and offering the kingdom to those who by the normal standards of Judaism were wicked.

We can clearly state what repentance would normally have involved. By ordinary Jewish standards, offenses against others required reparation as well as repentance. In Jesus' time, repentance would be demonstrated by sacrifice in the temple (e.g., Lev. 6:1–5). Jesus offered sinners inclusion in the kingdom not only *while* they were still sinners but also *without* requiring repentance. Therefore he could have been accused of being a friend of people who remained sinners. For Jesus to welcome repentant sinners who had made amends, would have been quite acceptable to the "righteous"—whatever else they may

have thought of Jesus. The scandal was that he associated
with sinners and rejoiced in their company. He asked only
that they accept his message—which offered them the
kingdom. This was the scandal of the righteous.[10] If Jesus
did recommend repentance he understood it, in the manner of the prophets, as total devotion to God. On the
whole, in contrast to the Baptist, he preached forgiveness
rather than repentance. And he turned forgiveness into
celebration (Luke 15:7, 10, 22–24, 32; 23:43).

Forgiveness

If Jesus' teaching on God's unmeasured forgiveness
was scandal to the righteous of his day, it was equally
unpalatable to many early Christians. Indeed, "sinners" are
hard to find in the early Church. A high tolerance for sinners was not characteristic of the early Church as far as we
know it. How, then, are we to understand Jesus' call to sinners in light of the fact that the Church seems not to have
continued the practice of admitting them? That Jesus
came to *call* the wicked was transformed into the belief
that he *died to save* sinners from sin. This is what the early
Church made of Jesus' call to sinners: that their behavior
should exceed the normal requirements of Judaism.
"Unless your righteousness exceeds that of the scribes and
the Pharisees, you will never enter the kingdom of heaven"
(Matt. 5:20).

While it was accepted that the risen Jesus had sent his followers to preach repentance and to baptize for the remission of sin, many within the community came to believe that the act of repentance or conversion, sealed by baptism, was accomplished once for all. Thus, the view developed that it was impossible to renew the grace received in baptism. The sins of apostasy and murder, and deviations from Christian standards of sexual morality, were regarded as the outcome of deliberate renunciation of the Christian way of life. For people who had committed these sins there could be no hope of forgiveness. Christ's death and resurrection had taken place once for all, and since Christian baptism involved entering into his once-for-all death and resurrection, baptism too must be once for all, so that its benefits could be given only once and, if renounced, could not be restored. Human logic had prevailed over divine forgiveness! (see Matt. 18:21–22, 23–35).

The author of Hebrews took a sternly rigoristic view. He is writing about apostasy:

> For it is impossible to restore again to repentance those who have once been enlightened, and have tasted the heavenly gift, and have become sharers in the Holy Spirit, and have tasted the goodness of the word of God and the powers of the age to come, and then have fallen away, since on their

own they are crucifying again the Son of God and
are holding him up to contempt. (6:4–6)

For if we wilfully persist in sin after having
received the knowledge of the truth, there no
longer remains a sacrifice for sins, but a fearful
prospect of judgment, and a fury of fire that will
consume the adversaries. Anyone who has violated
the law of Moses dies without mercy on the testi-
mony of two or three witnesses. How much worse
punishment do you think will be deserved by
those who have spurned the Son of God, profaned
the blood of the covenant by which they were
sanctified, and outraged the Spirit of grace . . . ? It
is a fearful thing to fall into the hands of the living
God. (10:26–29, 31)

The passages are painfully self-evident. Another is less
obvious:

For you know that later, when [Esau] wanted to
inherit the blessing, he was rejected, for he found
no chance to repent, even though he sought it with
tears. (12:17)

The reference is to Esau's sale of his birthright (Gen.
25:29–34), and the background is a Jewish tradition of

Esau's radical wickedness (not the biblical assumption). For the author of Hebrews, Esau stands as a frightening example of the irreversible result of immoral or irreligious conduct on the part of the elect.

The matter did not end with Hebrews—it remained a live issue. In summary, we must conclude that

> in the first three centuries there was a keen debate whether baptized believers who committed the capital sins of apostasy, impurity and bloodshed were admissible to reconciliation in this life. Almost without exception, the great christian writers of the second and early third centuries sided with the rigorists and refused reconciliation.[11]

So much for the teaching and praxis of Jesus!

Does God Really Forgive?

Our look at the stance of the early Church shows that one of the things about God we humans find very hard to accept is the depth and breadth of his forgiveness. "I'll forgive . . . but I can't forget!" is too often the measure of our forgiveness. We know that total, generous forgiveness of an injury, a hurt, asks very much of us. And we feel that, somehow, this must be so of God. Here, again, is another danger of our God-language. By necessity, we speak of

God in human terms. We tend to forget that such language is always analogical. Out of our human experience we can make statements about God. We need always to remind ourselves that what we say of God goes wholly *beyond* that experience. We understand forgiveness, but we cannot know *divine* forgiveness. When we temper the forgiveness of God by the standard of our forgiveness, we get it wrong. It is not theory only. It is distressing to find people, no longer young, who have lived a decent Christian life, often as religious, who still nurse a fear that, one fine day, their sins will be thrown back in their face. They have been forgiven; that much they accept. But there is the suspicion that God is holding in reserve his word of reproach. The robust faith of the prophets may bring encouragement. Isaiah carries a prayer attributed to King Hezekiah after he had been snatched from the brink of death. It has the hopeful word: "It was for my welfare that I had great bitterness. . . . for you have cast all my sins behind your back" (Isa. 38:17). Micah, in his lament for Zion, declares:

> Who is a God like you, pardoning iniquity, and passing over transgressions? . . . He will again have compassion upon us, he will tread our iniquities under foot. You will cast all our sins into the depths of the sea. (Mic. 7:18–19)

What powerful images! What mighty consolation! "You have cast all my sins behind your back": you have snatched them from me, you have cast them behind, thrown them over your shoulder, and have walked on without a backward glance. "He will tread our iniquities under foot": he will cover them over deeply and firmly, will bury them forever from his sight. "You will cast all our sins into the depths of the sea": you will lift the crushing burden that wears us down and sink it in the murky deep where such dark things belong.

This is the prophets' image of divine forgiveness, wholehearted forgiveness worthy of their God. Only Jesus could do better with his unforgettable picture of the loving Father who, without question and without condition, reinstates his errant son (Luke 15:20–24). We who are so generous in depicting the stern justice of God are so miserly in painting his love and mercy. It seems that we cannot abide a God who is more truly human than we are.

The Loving Father

In Chapter 15 of his gospel, Luke tells how Jesus reacted to the complaint of the pharisees and scribes that he "welcomes sinners and even eats with them." Jesus' reply was that he consorted with sinners precisely because he knew that God was a loving Father who welcomes the repentant sinner. The parables of the Lost Sheep and Lost Coin carry the moral: God will rejoice over even one sinner who repents. Both parables show the conversion of a sinner from God's point of view: he rejoices because he can forgive. The sheep and the coin represent the sinner who repents (a deed not easily achieved by sheep or coin). Hence the Prodigal Son—better, the Lost Boy— with human characteristics. For that matter, it is likely that the emphasis on repentance is Luke's qualification. Repentance would have been, at most, implicit in Jesus' words.

The story of father and sons (Luke 15:11–32) is allegory: the characters being God, the sinner, and the righteous. Jesus' Jewish hearers would have grasped the pathos of the young man's plight: a Jew herding pigs! He had hit rock bottom. What they would have found disconcerting was the incredible conduct of the father. That father represents God eagerly looking for the first steps of homecoming. After that initial turning on the part of a sinner, the action is all his. The son had gone away as son and had come back a pitiful tramp. Yet, he was reinstated without obligation; he is his son as though he had never left. And it is an occasion for rejoicing. Such is *God's* forgiveness.

In contrast, the attitude of the elder brother was effective armor against the plea of vulnerability and the foolishness of love. He had never really known his father, and now he rejects his brother. The story ends with an invitation: the elder son is invited to acknowledge his brother and enter into the joy of homecoming. Only so will he know his father as *Father*.

On many counts this is disturbing story for us
Christians of today. Luke took it out of the ministry of
Jesus and addressed it directly to the pharisees in his own
Christian community. And, surely, we must look to ourselves, to our possible resentment toward God's graciousness to sinners. We can find comfort in the warm treat-
ment of the younger son. Always, there is the father. He is
the real challenge. Our gracious and forgiving God holds
the stage.

This story persuasively shows God's loving concern for
humankind and, in particular, his favoritism toward the
outcast. It sets a question mark against the theology of forgiveness reflected in much of our penitential practice:
God's forgiveness seems too good to be true. Above all,
there is the uncomfortable message that one really comes
to understand this Father only by acknowledging the
brother and sister as brother and sister—a lesson learned
by the author of 1 John: "Those who do not love a brother
or sister whom they have seen cannot love the God whom
they have not seen" (4:20).

Response to Forgiveness

There remains the central reality of forgiveness. Too
often, God's deed is set in a grim context of reparation that
strips it of its graciousness. What ought to follow on forgiveness is loving response. Luke touchingly reveals this in

his story of "a woman in the city who was a sinner" (7:36–50). She was a woman who had previously encountered Jesus and had received his forgiveness. She made a brave and extravagant gesture: she kissed the feet of a reclining Jesus, to the evident scandal of his pharisee host. Jesus accepted her presence and ministering with gentle courtesy. And his verdict was clear and to the point: "Her great love proves that her sins have been forgiven" (7:47). One is not casual in the face of forgiveness. But response is not by way of "making up" to an offended deity.

Acknowledgment of forgiveness received can be expressed in other ways than the anointing of the feet of Jesus. The best way of all is by extension of forgiveness to others. In Matthew's Parable of the Unmerciful Servant, we meet again the sinner and his God (Matt. 18:13–35). An impossible debt is casually written off in response to the sinner's plea. And the man is not even penalized. Like the younger son in Jesus' parable, he is forgiven with no strings attached. Faced with a cry of desperation, the forgiving God was moved with pity (18:27). But when the recipient of such forgiveness cannot find it in his heart to be merciful, the Master is angry (18:33). Response to God's gracious forgiveness cannot be payment of a debt that is already fully remitted. It is, instead, warm thanksgiving for the blessing of such forgiving love. And the story in Matthew underlines again that sin, as God regards it, is man's inhumanity to man—whatever shape that may

take. Our abuse of others (and of ourselves) is an affront
to the loving Father who counts us as his children. Jesus
clearly understood this because he knew his Father.

One New Testament writer aptly described this God:

> When the goodness and loving kindness of God
> our Savior appeared, he saved us, not because of
> any works of righteousness that we had done, but
> according to his mercy, through the water of
> rebirth and renewal by the Holy Spirit. This Spirit
> he poured out upon us richly through Jesus Christ
> our Savior, so that having been justified by his
> grace, we might become heirs according to the
> hope of eternal life. (Titus 3:4–7)

Conclusion

In the first three chapters of Romans, Paul has painted
the state of humankind without God's gracious deed in
Christ. It is the backdrop to the heartening declaration:
"God proves his love for us in that while we still were sinners Christ died for us" (Rom. 5:8). We stand in need of
redemption. God alone can redeem us, can set us free. We
must turn to him, give him an opening. If we let him, he
will transform our lives. God calls us to *metanoia*, a change
of heart. But only he can bring about that change of heart.

He yearns to set us free from any and every slavery and bring us back into the shelter of his benign lordship. He asks for *faith,* and faith is nothing other than our "yes" to God. It is our willingness to let God *be* God in our lives. God awaits our consent. This is repentance.

Forgiveness does not come lightly. An offense is all the more hurtful if inflicted by one near and dear. In our human way we think it reasonable that forgiveness be shrouded in conditions; we expect reparation of some sort. This is not to suggest that forgiveness may not be whole-hearted and sincere. And there is the fact that, humanly speaking, and with the best intention, it is simply not easy to *forget* a deep hurt. The reminder of it is within us, in our very being.

We have, unhappily, tended to imagine divine forgiveness in terms of a human model. Indeed, consistent with our human image of God, we assume such forgiveness is reluctant: an offended deity is ready to forgive, provided he gets his pound of flesh. It is a sad travesty of God's forgiveness, yet one that is prevalent. Our Parent forgives, eagerly, wholly, if we give him the chance. "I will arise and go to my Father": a turning to him is all he asks. He—and he alone—can and will do the rest. To seek God's forgiveness is a homecoming; to be forgiven is to be welcomed home. It is a joyous moment, to be savored and celebrated.

5

Talking with God

While the primal command to "have dominion" gave no mandate for human dominion over humans, such dominion soon became a distinctive feature of human culture. Moreover, authority structures, civil and religious, invoked the sanction of the gods—or of God. It was assumed that God had issued to the establishment a blank check. God was seen as champion of the privileged, upholder of the status quo.

Fortunately, a challenge was mounted in Israel: God is not the God of the Establishment; he is not a sustainer of unjust systems. God had longed for this challenge. He waited because he would not use force. Wearied by passive subservience and pained by a religion that invoked him in support of oppression, he welcomed those who challenged the false god foisted on them. He rejoiced that there were children of his who understood him and who recognized him. He stepped by the "great" and welcomed those who cried out to him against the popular caricature.

Talking Back to God

We tend to be inhibited and formulistic in our prayer. We imagine that there is an appropriate manner of addressing God—a refined and courtly language befitting divinity. We expect God to conduct himself in a proper "godly" manner, and we assume that he wants us to be "proper" in our approach to him. We learn from the Old Testament that Israel, with a more robust understanding of God, could dare to complain of God to God, could talk back at him without constraint, could even try blackmailing him. Some instances may open our eyes to this refreshing trend.

Moses

Moses was a leader and a mediator. Conscious of his role of intercessor, he was outspoken and generous. But when he was sent to free his people, he found that his approach to the Pharaoh seemed only to aggravate their plight. In exasperation, he complained: "You have done nothing at all to deliver your people!" (Exod. 5:23). Later, when the people were delivered from Egyptian slavery, Moses learned, painfully, of human fickleness. The people, scared by this sudden freedom, yearned for security, and turned against Moses and God. Moses was prepared to put his neck on the block. If Yahweh would not forgive the people's infidelity, then: "Blot me, I pray you, out of your book that you have written" (32:32). He reminded God that these unfaithful left in his charge were *God's* people—*he* might try looking after them for a change! (33:12–13). Yahweh called his bluff. He proposed to destroy the rebellious people and make Moses father of a new people, but Moses would have none of it (Num. 14:13–19). Already we catch that comforting interplay. God has a sense of humor and matches our human posturing, not with condescension but with gracious, if humorous, respect. He is a Parent who does not talk down to his children.

Jeremiah

Jeremiah was a prophet who never wanted to be a prophet. To make matters worse, because of the appalling political and religious situation of his day, he was a prophet of doom. His mission was "to pluck up and to pull down, to destroy and to overthrow" (Jer. 1:10), to cry out, without respite, "violence and destruction" against the people he loved (20:8). The so-called Confessions are a record of Jeremiah's communing with God and are central for an understanding of Jeremiah (11:18–12:6; 15:10–21; 17:12–18; 18:18–23; 20:7–18). Not only are they fascinating because they permit us to gaze into the heart of a prophet, they are encouraging because they let us see how very human the prophet was. His prophetic office was burdensome, a burden that seems to have been heavier and more painful than that of any other prophet. And he cried out at the unfairness of it. He cried out in confidence that God could cope with all that he might throw at God. We have imagined an angry God. What we find in Jeremiah is a very angry prophet. He could, and did, complain:

> I did not sit in the company of merrymakers, nor did I rejoice; under the weight of your hand I sat alone. . . . Why is my pain unceasing, my wound incurable, refusing to be healed? Truly you are to me like a deceitful brook, like waters that fail. (15:17–18; see 14:8–9)

Jeremiah's vocation set him apart; he could not be as other men. He felt the lonely pang of his calling. His only companion was the Lord he served—and would even he abandon him? Was God nothing more than a mirage? A cry of faith, shot through with so much pain.

Behold, they say to me, "Where is the word of the Lord? Let it come!" I have not pressed you to send evil, nor have I desired the day of disaster—as you know. That which came out of my lips was your word. (17:15–16)

Again, we hear the burden of the prophetic office. Jeremiah found no pleasure in being a prophet of doom; he did not enjoy being the butt of sarcasm and sneering. He did no more than hear faithfully and proclaim courageously the word of the Lord. And he suffered because of his intense sympathy with the people over whom he proclaimed the judgment of God. "O Lord, you have deceived me, and I was deceived; you are stronger than I, and you have prevailed. I have become a laughing-stock all day long; everyone mocks me" (20:7). This is truly marvelous. Let us look at what Jeremiah implied when he declared: "you are stronger than I." What he said in effect was: "Yahweh, you are a great big bully!" He had enough, and he told his God so in no uncertain terms. For Jeremiah, God was so real, so personal, that he could speak out to him—and at him—with outrageous boldness. The decisive factor was that Jeremiah could do so from a position of strength. He was a prophet who, no matter how hard it went, was unflinchingly faithful to the service God had asked of him.

Job

Job is an outstanding example of challenge with his harrowing journey from faith to faith. It was an epic journey, though he had not stirred from his seat on the ash-heap. He groped through a dark night, throwing down the gauntlet to that elusive God along the way. His quest for an answer to the perennial problem of innocent suffering is as pressing in our day as it was in his. The dominant theology of his day, represented by his theologian "friends," Eliphaz, Bildad, Zophar, was that *all* suffering is a result of sin. There is no innocent suffering. Besides, it was believed, there is exact retribution: virtue is rewarded, wickedness is punished—*in this life*. For, at the age of the Book of Job, in Israel, there was no concept of life after death. Job looked, dispassionately, at life and declared with candor:

It is all one; therefore I say
he destroys both the blameless and the wicked.
When disaster brings sudden death,
he mocks at the calamity of the innocent. (9:22–23)

This is an honest reaction to the unfairness of life. If, for us, with our belief in an afterlife and a realm where discrepancies may be sorted out, injustice in our world is still so painful, what must it have been for those, like the

author of Job, for whom there was no afterlife? Personally,
I feel humble before the Book of Job. Not only because it
is a literary and theological masterpiece (a remarkable
achievement, this marriage of poetry and theology) but
because Job was a believer who could sustain faith in a caring God when all experience pointed in another direction.
His problem is highlighted in the outrageous passage
where Job asked, in exasperation: "Why are not times of
judgment kept by the Almighty?" (24:1–12). Why is God
not just? Job had, before, subscribed to the theology that
said *all* suffering is due to sin. His experience showed this
theology to be wholly wrong. We (the readers) know that
Job's plea of innocence was authentic (Job 1–2). Neither
Job nor his theologian friends were let in on the secret. Job
experienced that the theology did not work. In their theoretical ivory tower they diagnosed Job's problem: he suffers
because he is a sinner. The Book of Job is, and will always
be, a radical challenge to any theology that seeks to oper-
ate outside of experience. Indeed, the author has bril-
liantly devastated any neat theological system. The three
theologians had seen themselves as champions of God,
defending his cause against the "heretic" Job. At the close,
there is the shock: "My wrath is kindled against you. . . .
for you have not spoken of me what is right, as my servant
Job has" (Job 42:7). The author twists the knife as he has
the orthodox theologians forgiven by God at the interces-
sion of the heretic (42:8–9). They had pushed the cause of

their God, a theoretical God. And Job rebelled: he sought
the true God. Later, Jesus would be declared a heretic, precisely because he proclaimed *his* God against every caricature of him. He ended up nailed to a cross. It is always
dangerous to proclaim the *true* God.

Psalm 88

Perhaps the most mind-boggling cry to God is in
Psalm 88 or, at least, in the core of the psalm. It boils
down to an unmitigated accusation of God.

> You have laid me in the depths of the tomb,
> in places that are dark, in the depths.
> your anger weighs down upon me:
> I am drowned beneath your waves.

> You have taken away my friends
> and made me hateful in their sight.
> Imprisoned, I cannot escape;
> my eyes are sunken with grief.

> As for me, Lord, I call to you for help:
> in the morning my prayer comes before you.
> Lord, why do you reject me?
> Why do you hide your face?

> Wretched, close to death from my youth,
> I have borne your trials, I am numb.
> Your fury has swept down upon me;
> your terrors have utterly destroyed me.
>
> Friend and foe you have taken away,
> my one companion is darkness.

It is helpful to read the psalm, and then to reread it. Here is one who has had a wholly unhappy life ("from my youth"). He has had enough and cries out to God. The startling factor is the accusative "you." All his misery is laid at the door of God. Look at it: The psalmist echoes the accusation of Jeremiah (Jer. 20:7): God is a bully! *You* have caused all my sufferings, *you* have turned my friends against me, *your* fury rains upon me. I have prayed to you, but you don't hear. The implication: Get your act together, God; I have had it! But, just as with Job, this is a cry of faith. What we learn is that God is not happy with sycophants. He may not be too comfortable with the righteous. But, he exults in those who take him seriously enough to fight with him. These are people who *do* believe.

Prayers of the Chastened

Laments, or prayers, call them what you will. There is, however, another very different way of talking to God. It is one thing to challenge him from the point of at least striving to do his will. But when one is painfully conscious of having failed, even dismally, then what does one do? It seems to me that post-exilic prayers are an encouragement and a comfort. They are straightforward. We have sinned; we deserve all we received. Are we depressed? No! We acknowledge our sin, our shameful ingratitude—and we turn to God! *We* have done wrong; *we* have failed—but you are *you*! It is, in anticipation, "I shall arise, and go to my Father."

Trauma of Exile

Now the Lord said to Abram, "Go from your country and your kindred and your father's house to the land that I will show you. And I will make of you a great nation, and I will bless you, and make your name great." (Gen. 12:1–2)

I will raise up your son after you . . . and I will establish his kingdom . . . Your house and your kingdom shall be made sure for ever before me; your throne shall be established for ever. (2 Sam 7:12, 16)

What was an Israelite to think when God's solemn promise to Abraham and his word of assurance to David

had come to nothing? There was no questioning the harsh
reality of Nebuchadnezzar's conquest: temple, city, and
nation were gone. On the strength of Yahweh's word it
ought not have been so; but it had happened. For the
thoughtful Yahwist the disaster was a mirror held up to the
nation, a mirror that showed a visage of gross failure and
sin. Some, at least, had learned from the bitter experience
of the Babylonian Exile: the faith-answer to the disaster
was repentance and hope. The people had failed—of that
there could be no doubt. But Yahweh was faithful and
steadfast as ever. There was a way of restoration, a way of
redemption. It was the way of candid confession of sin and
of total trust in God's boundless mercy. The many moving
post-exilic prayers to be found in Lamentations and
Baruch, Ezra and Nehemiah, Tobit and Sirach, Esther and
Judith and the Book of Daniel firmly follow this way.[12]

While post-exilic prayers tend to be lengthy, there is
about them a refreshing candor and an inspiring faith in
them. They are the prayers of a chastened people, a people that, in adversity, had found its soul. Those who pray
openly confess sin, yet maintain a quiet dignity. Most
instructive is a recurring phrase that characterizes God as
"the great and terrible God who keeps covenant and steadfast love with those who love him and keep his commandments"—followed always by the confession: "We
have sinned." These later Israelites have come to know
that "the great and terrible God" is such only to those who

have never known him. Those who pray those prayers have discovered the way of restoration, the way of redemption.

Hopeful Confession

Characteristic of these post-exilic prayers is confession of sin. But, if there is the admission that "Jerusalem sinned grievously" (Lam. 1:8) with the inevitable result that "the Lord has become like an enemy, he has destroyed Israel" (2:5), there is also the serene assurance:

> For the Lord will not reject forever.
> Although he causes grief, he will have compassion
> according to the abundance of his steadfast love;
> for he does not willingly afflict or grieve anyone.
> (Lam. 3:31–33)

Even in such deep distress, the heartening note of complaint still sounds:

> Why have you forgotten us completely?
> Why have you forsaken us these many days?
> Restore us to yourself, O Lord,
>   that we may be restored!
> Renew our days as of old —
> unless you have utterly rejected us,
> and are angry with us beyond measure. (5:20–22)

"Have you utterly rejected us?" It is not just a rhetorical question. It carries overtones of exasperation worthy of Moses or Jeremiah. Here is a people bloodied but un-bowed—not in defiance of God but in robust confidence in his loving kindness.

Another appendix to Jeremiah is Baruch. Its writer is very conscious of the glaring contrast between the holy God and his sinful people: "The Lord our God is in the right, but there is open shame on us and our ancestors this very day" (Bar. 2:6; see 1:15). The introduction to this prayer (1:15–2:10) is a candid confession of sin: "We have not entreated the favor of the Lord by turning away, each of us, from the thoughts of our wicked hearts. . . . We have not obeyed his voice, to walk in the statutes of the Lord which he set before us" (Bar. 2:8, 10). The prayer itself (2:11–3:8) recalls the great Exodus event. That is the basis of the exiled people's confidence, not necessarily that they be restored to their homeland, but that in exile they may meet their God.

> O Lord Almighty, God of Israel, the soul in anguish and the wearied spirit cry out to you. Hear, O Lord, and have mercy, for we have sinned before you. . . . Do not remember the iniquities of our ancestors, but in this crisis remember your power and your name. For you are the Lord our God, and it is you, O Lord, whom we will praise.

For you have put the fear of you in our hearts so
that we would call upon your name; and we will
praise you in our exile, for we have put away from
our hearts all the iniquity of our ancestors who
sinned against you. (3:1–2, 5–7)

The epitome of these post-exilic prayers is in the Book
of Daniel (Dan. 9:4–19). This prayer is not only typical,
it is the most moving of all these prayers of the chastened.
But we would close with another prayer—the apocryphal
Prayer of Manasseh.

The Chronicler alone tells of Manasseh's conversion
and makes reference to his prayer of repentance (2 Chron.
33:10–19). A later writer supplied an appropriate prayer,
a worthy example of post-exilic piety, a prayer of repentance more moving than the Miserere (Ps. 51). Some
excerpts will make the point:

immeasurable and unsearchable is
    your promised mercy,
for you are the Lord Most High,
of great compassion, long-suffering,
    and very merciful. . . .
You, O Lord, according to your great goodness
have promised repentance and forgiveness
to those who have sinned against you;
and in the multitude of your mercies

you have appointed repentance for sinners,
that they may be saved. . . .
you have appointed repentance for me,
    who am a sinner. . . .
And now I bend the knee of my heart,
beseeching you for your kindness.
I have sinned, O Lord, I have sinned,
and I know my transgressions.
I earnestly beseech you,
forgive me, O Lord, forgive me!
For you, O Lord, are the God of those who repent,
and in me you will manifest your goodness;
for, unworthy as I am,
    you will save me in your great mercy,
and I will praise you continually all the days of my life.

If even Manasseh (who gets such a bad press in 2 Kings and Chronicles), after turning back to the Lord, could feel confident of salvation, there is hope for any and every sinner!

Conclusion

Our God is a robust God with a sense of humor. Too many make do with a humorless God—to their loss. Our God is not petty; he can take anything we throw at him. He rejoices when we get really angry with him, because then we *are* taking him seriously. The story of Jacob's wrestling with God (Gen. 32:24–32) is of profound spiritual significance. Jacob learned that a genuine relationship with God could not be a merely passive one; it entailed personal effort, striving, a wrestling with the divine will. Jacob matured in the struggle; his encounter with God transformed him. Up to that moment he was an unscrupulous manipulator, but afterwards he was a different Jacob.

God wants us to wrestle with him. And he wants us to complain, to cry out against injustice, wherever we find it. God wants dialogue with us. He wants us to talk *to* him; not, as we usually do, *past* him. And we address him most directly when we are in deep trouble or when we are good and angry. Then we are *talking with God.*

Of course, there is another side to it. Although we are children of God, we are *sinful* children. We have not responded fittingly to his goodness; we have taken advantage of his love. We are sorry, or ought to be, for our failures. But our God does not want us to feel *guilt.* He is a God of compassion who is with us in our sorrow. He is a God of forgiveness and his forgiveness is prompt and total. We, then, should have the decency—the humility—to acknowledge our failures: "God, be merciful to me, a sinner."

We do not grovel. We come before him with human dignity. We owe that not only to ourselves, but especially

to our Creator. It does not honor him for us to debase ourselves. After all, we are those for whose sake he did not
spare his own Son. We owe him the compliment of our
self-respect. If prayer is conversation with God, the ideal
prayer is a heart-to-heart chat of a loving Parent with a
child—a naughty child. That is implied in the challenge
of Jesus: "Unless you become like children." This does not
mean childishness but openness to receive—and the freedom to come, tear-stained, to our God for comfort.

6

Image of the Invisible God

To make our way to God, we must learn to accept that God has first made his way to us. The original sin was humankind's snatching at the wisdom that could only be gift (Gen. 3:1–7). Humanity's sin continues to be an attempt to escape the ways of God. It has long perplexed and disturbed me that Old Testament men and women often had a deeper understanding of God, and certainly a more personal relationship with God, than has been the experience of many Christians. In Jesus of Nazareth the divine has entered into our world, our history. God has become one among us. But we would bypass the way of God. The primal temptation is still there: "you will be like God." The basic Christian truth is: "I am the way" (John 14:6). If God's way to humankind is through the man

Jesus, then our Christian way to God is through the man Jesus.

Like Us in All Things

One New Testament writer who had come to terms theologically with the death of Jesus was the author of the Letter to the Hebrews. He thoroughly understood that the salvation of humankind could not be salvation *from* humanness but salvation *of* our humanness. After all, what is salvation? It means, surely, that I, a human person, become *fully* human—fully human as God had intended me to be. And salvation cannot be something outside our humanness; this would be no salvation at all. What has, in fact, come to pass is something intensely moving: God, in Jesus, reaching into our history of suffering and brokenness. "It was fitting that God, for whom and through whom all things exist, in bringing many children to glory, should make the pioneer of their salvation perfect through sufferings" (Heb. 2:10). God has made our cause his concern.

God Was in Christ

"God was in Christ, reconciling the world to himself" (2 Cor. 5:19). This is arguably the very best Christological statement, and it weds Christology with soteriology.

Where Jesus is, there is God; and God is there *for us*. But Jesus of Nazareth is the thoroughly human person who was "born of woman" (Gal. 4:4), who lived in our world, who died, horribly, on a cross. We cannot *know* God; yet, we meet God in Jesus. The author of Hebrews has told us in no uncertain terms: "When in times past God spoke to our forefathers, he spoke in many and varied ways through the prophets." This is revelation of God indeed, but fragmentary, and mediated through his *servants*. "In these last days he has spoken to us by his Son. . . . he is the reflection of God's glory, and the exact imprint of God's very being" (Heb. 1:1–3). This Son, who is the whole word of God, is the Jesus who "had to become like his brothers and sisters in every respect. . . . one who in every respect has been tested as we are, yet without sin" (2:17; 4:15).

If Jesus bears the stamp of God's very being, he does so as a human person, like us in all things. *Jesus* tells us what God is like. *Jesus* is God's summons to us, God's challenge to us. We can say, truly, that God is love; but we have no idea what *divine* love is in itself. In Jesus we see God's love in action. We learn that God is a God who is with us in our suffering and our death. We are sure of it because of the suffering and death of Jesus.

In Jesus, God has shown himself in human form: "he is the image of the invisible God" (Col. 1:15). In practice, we have slipped quickly past this human aspect. We have turned, instead, to a "divine icon" comfortably free of any trait of the critical prophet. We had consigned Jesus to his heavenly home. And wisely, because we had realized a long time ago that he is much safer there! We genuflect before "Our Divine Lord" who does not impinge on us because of the way we envision him: he does not really have any critical impact on the life of our world. But Jesus of Nazareth is a very uncomfortable person to have about, a constant challenge. For Christians, God is Father of our Lord Jesus Christ—our Lord who died on a cross.

Suffering and Death

Our human history, before the *eschaton* (the End), is one largely compounded of suffering. It is therefore "fitting" (Heb. 2:10) in accordance with the character of our God that in seeking to bring humankind to "glory," the destined End, in and through Jesus, he should have Jesus walk the road of human suffering. He has become *one of us,* sharing our sorrow and our anxiety, in order to be the first to reach perfection—the first to become *the true image* of God, the first *to become wholly human.* It is fitting that, trapped in a history of suffering, we should be set free by one who has entered into that suffering and made it his own (2:10). We can truly see God in the face of Jesus.

For the author of Hebrews Jesus is Son of God; but he is, as we have noted, the Son who "had to become like his brothers and sisters in every respect" (2:17), a Son who "in

every respect has been tested as we are, yet without sin"
(4:15). He is the human being who stands in a relationship of obedient faithfulness towards God (3:16) and who
stands in solidarity with human suffering. Thus he is
mediator: a true priest who can bring humankind to God.
If he bears "the exact imprint of God's very being" (1:3),
it is because we see in him what makes God God; he
shows us that God is God of humankind.

The author is surely aware of the pattern of the life of
Jesus; there are several pointers throughout his homily.
But, like Paul, he concentrates on the moment of death
(and exaltation). He finds the meaning of the life of Jesus
in his crucifixion—accepted as a self-sacrifice for broken
humankind. He had come to do the saving will of the
Father and had learned God's purpose in the "school of
suffering" (5:8). In Gethsemane he had prayed "with loud
cries and tears to the one who was able to save him from
death" (5:7). He came to understand that the way of faithfulness led to the cross.

The death of Jesus is presented as a bloody sacrifice,
with the accent on Jesus' self-surrender in this violent
death.[13] Because the sacrifice is the death of Jesus it
marked the end of his earthly life. Yet, the sacrifice of Jesus
did not end on the cross. By God's graciousness (Heb.
2:9), his death was for the benefit of all men and women.
The Father had seen in the death of Jesus the supreme
assertion of his love for humankind and his faithfulness

toward God—for we must always have in mind that the
meaning of Jesus' death is to be found in his life.
Exaltation to the right hand of the Father is the divine
recognition of the significance of the death of Jesus, giving
this death its abiding, eternal value.

God is revealed with unwonted clarity in one human
life and in one episode of human history. If Jesus is image
of the invisible God, the cross is revelation of true God
and true humankind. On the cross God shows what it is
to be human. God's Son dramatically demonstrates the
radical powerlessness of the human being. He shows us
that we are truly human when we accept our humanness,
when we face up to the fact that we are not masters of our
fate. The Cross offers the authentic definition of humanness: God's definition. There, he starkly and firmly
reminds us of who and what we are. On the cross God
defines the human being as creature—not to crush or
humiliate, but that he may be, as Creator, wholly with his
creature. On its own, humankind has indeed reason to
fear. With God, in total dependence on God, there is no
room for fear. The resurrection of Jesus makes that clear.
For the resurrection is God's endorsement of the definition of humankind established on the cross. And it is
God's endorsement of the definition of God established
there. He is the God who has entered, wholly, into rejection and humiliation and suffering. He is the God present
in human life where to human eyes he is absent: "My God,

my God, why have you forsaken me?" (Mark 15:34). He
is the God of humankind. He is God *for us*. The paradoxical triumph of the shameful death of Jesus is given force-
ful dramatic expression in the Book of Revelation.

The Lamb Who Was Slain

> One of the elders said to me: "Do not weep; the
> Lion from the tribe of Judah, the root of David,
> has won the right to open the scroll and its seven
> seals." Then I saw between the throne and the four
> living creatures and among the elders a Lamb
> standing as though it had been slain. (Rev 5:5–6)

The Lamb

In the Book of Revelation the emergence of the
Lamb—John's definitive title for Christ—is dramatic even
in the context of this dramatic book. The significant factor is that he is the *slain* Lamb. In his vision of the heavenly throne-room, John had been bidden to look for the
Lion of the tribe of Judah. What met his gaze was "a Lamb
standing as though it had been slain." A surprise, surely—
but should we have been taken by surprise? After all,
John's first characterization of Jesus Christ was as the one
"who loves us and has loosed us from our sins with his

blood" (1:5). Indeed, these very words are now caught up in the heavenly canticle: "you were slain and by your blood you bought for God people from every nation" (5:9).

If "Lamb" was John's favorite title for Christ, one may not forget that, from the outset, he was the Lamb who was slain. When John proceeds to paint the power and triumph of the Lamb, he is clear and wants it understood that the decisive victory of the Lamb was won on the cross. He had made his own the conviction of Paul: "We proclaim Christ crucified . . . Christ the power of God and the wisdom of God. For God's foolishness is wiser than human wisdom, and God's weakness is stronger than human strength" (1 Cor 1:23–25). It is precisely in view of the "foolishness" of God that John hears the heavenly celebration of the slain Lamb as one worthy to receive all power (5:21), as one worthy of honor side by side with the One on the throne (5:13).

"Then one of the elders *said* to me . . . the Lion of the tribe of Judah . . . has conquered . . . I *saw* a Lamb standing, as though it had been slain" (Rev. 5:5–6). In his vision John looked for the emergence of a Lion—and saw a slaughtered Lamb! What he learned, and what he tells his readers, is that the Lion is the Lamb: the ultimate power of God ("lion") is manifest on the Cross ("lamb"). This is why "Lamb" is John's definitive name for Christ. Operating by the ultimate power of God, the Lamb conquers: to conquer (*nikaō*) is John's definitive Christological verb. To conquer, in the case of Christ and Christians, is to die. Throughout Revelation "conquer" never designates vindictive action against the enemies of Christ or Christians. Jesus, silent before the Roman procurator, faithful unto death, won his victory.

The Lamb had won the right to break the seven seals. He went to the throne to receive from the hand of the One on the throne the scroll: a transfer of power (Rev. 5). God had waited for an agent through whom his purpose for humankind would unfold. He had found him in the slain and risen Lamb. Our Almighty God manifests his might in the Cross. In the Cross, through the blood of the Lamb, he offers forgiveness and holds out salvation to all. There is only one answer to the evil that is sin, and to all evil. Violence can never be the answer. Despite the plagues of Revelation (plagues in vision only), it is not God's answer. Nothing but love, the infinitely patient divine love, can absorb evil and put it out of commission. The Cross shows the earnestness of a gracious God, shows that there is no limit to his desire to win humankind to himself. The Lamb as the manifestation, as the very presence, of our gracious God, is worthy of honor and worship. He is worthy precisely as the slain Lamb, as the crucified One. In John's view, God's victory has been won: on the Cross. Jesus conquered through suffering and weakness rather than by might. Hence the paradox that, in Christian terms, the Victim is the Victor.

The Faithful Witness

A distinctive feature of John's presentation of the Lamb is his assimilation of the Lamb to God. The multitude of the saved attribute their victory to God "and the Lamb" (Rev. 7:10). The heavenly Jerusalem has no temple— "its temple was the Lord God Almighty and the Lamb"; and the Lamb is the lamp of the heavenly city (21:22–23). When the Throne (symbol of God throughout) appears for the last time, now in the City-Temple, it is "the throne of God and of the Lamb" (22:1, 3). Accordingly, the Lamb can declare of himself: "I am the Alpha and the Omega, the first and the last, the beginning and the end" (22:13)—echoing the words of the One on the throne (21:6). In short, one might have the Lamb speak as does the Johannine Jesus: "I and the Father are one" (John 10:30).

The parallel is instructive. The Johannine Jesus is one with the Father precisely because he is the one sent, the agent of the Father, and is thereby empowered to speak the words of God. John's Lamb is the "faithful witness" (Rev. 1:5) who has received his revelation from God (1:1). It is because of his faithfulness to his witness-bearing, a faithfulness that brought him to the Cross, that he shares the throne of God. It is no less clear to the Lamb than it is to the Johannine Jesus that "the Father is greater than I" (John 14:28); the one sent and the faithful witness have this in common. They also share the declaration: "He who has seen me has seen the Father" (John 14:9). "I and the Father are one . . . the throne of God and of the Lamb"— these tell us nothing of the "nature" of the Son/Lamb but tell us everything of the role of Revealer that is the role of the Son/Lamb. For John, Jesus is the one in whom God is fully present. God is the one who reveals himself wholly in Jesus.

We know God through human perception of God. That perception will always be culturally conditioned; it will be colored by the human and historical situation. As a Christian, John saw his God revealed in the Lamb who was slain. That truth colored his vision of the One on the throne. He would not seek to describe that God, so far beyond any conception of human majesty. Yet, this was no aloof God. He was the God present in the Son. John had been loosed from sin in the blood of that Son. He had experienced the love of God. Never, for him, could God be a distant God. This awareness, indeed, was not something wholly new. As a Jew, sensitive to the prophetic tradition, he had been familiar with the reality of a transcendent God immersed in the life of his people. The Christ—the presence of God—who walks among John's Churches (Chs. 2–3) plays the role that Yahweh had played through his prophets.

The majestic, awesome One who sits on the throne is the same One who has revealed himself in the Lamb. It is this fact that makes acceptable the otherwise repellent violent imagery of Revelation. As do biblical writers in general, John had to strive to convey in inadequate human language what limited human minds cannot comprehend in the first place. Our Creator God is a Saving God. He is the God who desires to set humankind free from the tyranny of sin and evil. He is a God grieved by the ravages of evil—*that* is his "wrath." He cannot and will not ignore sin and evil. "The people of Israel groaned under their bondage . . . and God heard their groaning" (Exod. 2:23–24). He will not turn a blind eye to oppression and to the travail of the oppressed. The violent imagery and language are designed to underline this truth. In human terms, there is retribution.

"Pay [Rome] back in her own coin, repay her twice over for her works. In the cup she mixed, mix her a double draught!" (Rev. 18:6). The sentiment is human; God's "retribution" is divine. "God so loved the world that he gave his only Son" (John 3:16); "God proves his love for us in that while we were still sinners Christ died for us" (Rom. 5:8). It is this God who is revealed in the Lamb who was slain. The decisive battle in God's war against Evil will not be at Armageddon; it *was fought on the cross.* If war in heaven is a repercussion of that victorious battle (Rev. 12:7–12), strife on earth is a reflection of it. That is the challenge to John's disciples and to all believers: "In the world you will have tribulation; but take courage; I have conquered the world!" (John 16:33). It is not easy to discern evident signs of God's total victory in the manifest evils of our world. Faith must find ways of asserting it. But our human ways must always fall very short of painting the reality. It is helpful to recall the sage observation of Claus Westermann apropos of Genesis 1:31: "And God saw everything that he had made, and indeed, it was very good."

> It was God's judgment that creation was good. It can never be our judgment, the fruit of our own experience. Our knowledge and experience are always limited by the unexplained and the incomprehensible. We can speak about creation then only with reference to the creator for whom it presents no riddle.[14]

Graciousness

In relation to his own, the Lamb displays all the graciousness of God. He has liberated us from the evil deeds of our past. He has purchased from slavery, for God, at the cost of his blood, men and women of every nation, making of them a royal house of priests (Rev. 5:9). The victors, who have come through the great tribulation, have won their victory in virtue of his—they have washed their robes in the blood of the Lamb (7:14). He is the Shepherd who will guide them to the water of life (7:17). The victors share in the victory of the Lamb over the Dragon—they have conquered him by the blood of the Lamb (12:10–11). They are the faithful ones, marked with the name of the Lamb and of his Father (14:1–5), who "follow the Lamb wherever he goes" (14:4). As first fruits of the harvest of the world they represent the whole Church, all those ransomed from the earth. They are those who have been fondly harvested by the one "like a son of man"—the gracious Lamb (14:14–16). The companions of the Lamb are the "armies of heaven" who accompany him, now as invincible Rider on the white horse, as he rides out to final victory (19:11–21). One may see here the fourth evangelist's triumphal portrayal of the passion and death of Jesus pushed to the limit of apocalyptic imagery. There is the lovelier image of the marriage of the Lamb. The Victors are invited to his marriage supper. In the exuberance of John's imagery, guests and Bride are one and the same (19:7–9). It is the consummation of the Lamb's—and therefore of God's—love affair with humankind. The imagery first put forth in Hosea 1–3 now, in Revelation, comes to full flowering. Truly, "God's dwelling is with humankind" (21:3).

No sketch of the Lamb would be complete without a glance at the Lord of the Churches. The title Lamb is not used for Christ in Chapters 2–3, but he is that heavenly scrutinizer. As "one in human form," he is seen in striking majesty—he is *the* Victor. John falls, in helpless awe, at his feet—to hear the reassuring voice of the Jesus of the gospel: "Do not be afraid." John realizes that here is no stranger. And he is no absentee landlord: he walks among the Churches. His message to each community is incisive and decisive. He looks at the state of each. He finds love, faithfulness even to death, patient endurance in the face of intolerance and persecution. And he finds failure in love, a willingness to compromise with an inimical world, and the danger of betrayal. Always there is glowing promise to the Victors, those who hold steadfast to the end.[15]

Conclusion

Jesus is image of the invisible God. Jesus is uniquely Son of God as Hebrews had declared him to be. Jesus' divinity is not, as sometimes presented, some kind of second substance in him. His divinity consists in the fact that he is Jesus, the manifestation and presence of God in our world. Any misperception that "Jesus is human, but . . ." (and it is all too common) is, effectively, rejection of the God who revealed himself in Jesus. When the human Jesus is not acknowledged, our understanding of God suffers and our Christianity suffers. This is not to say that the whole reality of Jesus may be adequately summed up under the title "human being"—there is something other, something much more. But his human wholeness must be acknowledged. Jesus was not interested in saving "souls" (happily, his anthropology was not dualistic); he was concerned with *people*. In relation to women, given the culture of his day, he was unconventional. His band of disciples was a mixed group of men and women. Jesus was the *friend* of sinners—he brought hope into their lives. It is only by taking with utmost seriousness the humanness of Jesus that one may acknowledge God as a *Deus humanissimus,* a God bent on the salvation of humankind. Any other God is not the Father of our Lord Jesus Christ—the God of Christians.

Notes

1. Penny Livermore, *Called to His Supper* (Wilmington: M. Glazier, 1978), 25. See also Psalm 34:1–10.

2. Benjamin Whichcote, *Select Notions* (London: 1685), 115.

3. Edward Schillebeeckx, *Jesus in Our Western Culture: Mysticism, Ethics and Politics* (London: SCM, 1987), 14.

4. *The Epistle of Paul to the Romans* (London: Collins, 1959), 55.

5. Schillebeeckx, *op. cit.,* 5–6.

6. Edward Schillebeeckx, *God Among Us. The Gospel Proclaimed* (New York: Crossroad, 1983), 94. See also 91–102.

7. See Claus Westermann, *Genesis 1–11. A Commentary* (Minneapolis/London: Augsburg/SPCK, 1984), 269–78.

8. Paul Gallico, *Thomasina* (Middleton: Penguin Books, 1987), 146.

9. *Church. The Human Story of God* (London: SCM, 1990), 117.

10. See E. P. Sanders, *Jesus and Judaism* (London: SCM, 1985), 174–211; James D. G. Dunn, *Jesus, Paul and the Law* (London: SPCK, 1990), 79–81; Wilfrid Harrington, *The Tears of God* (Collegeville, MN: The Liturgical Press, 1992), 42–44.

11. James J. Walter in J. Komonchak, M. Collins, D. Lane (eds.), *The New Dictionary of Theology* (Wilmington: M. Glazier, 1987), 876.

12. Lam. 1–5; Bar. 1:15–3:8; Ezra 9:6–15; Neh. 1:5–11; 9:6–37; Tob. 13:1–8; Sir. 36:1–17; Esther 13:9–17; 14:3–19; Jth. 9:2–14; Dan. 3:26–45; 9:4–19.

13. Consider how perverse it is that later theology went on to explain the death of Jesus in terms of Old Testament sacrifice—while Hebrews is singlemindedly concerned with demonstrating that our High Priest has transcended and replaced the whole Old Testament cultic system. We thereby made so many difficulties for ourselves.

14. *Op. cit.,* 174–75.

15. See Wilfrid J. Harrington, *Revelation.* Sacra Pagina series (Collegeville, MN: The Liturgical Press, 1993).